Soul Wounds

The Ties that Bind.

Navigating Sibling Rivalry and Healing.

Publisher Awareherness Press Publishers

Awareherness@gmail.com

ISBN: 978-1-965702-09-3

Dear Beautiful Soul,

Welcome to "Soul Wounds: The Ties That Bind." This journal is your sacred space for reflection, healing, and connection as you explore the complexities of sibling relationships.

Here, you will have the opportunity to:

Reflect on your experiences with your siblings.
Explore the emotions tied to rivalry and love.
Heal old wounds and foster empathy.
Grow closer to your siblings through open communication.

Take your time filling these pages, and let your heart guide your pen. There is no right or wrong way to express your thoughts and feelings in this safe space.

As a 10x Best-Selling Author and recipient of the International Impact Book Award, I believe in the transformative power of self-reflection. May this journal be a catalyst for understanding and healing in your relationships..

Awareherness begins now.

With warmth,
Dr. Kellie Diane

Self Reflection and Awareness

Day: 1

Describe your relationship with you and all of
your siblings.

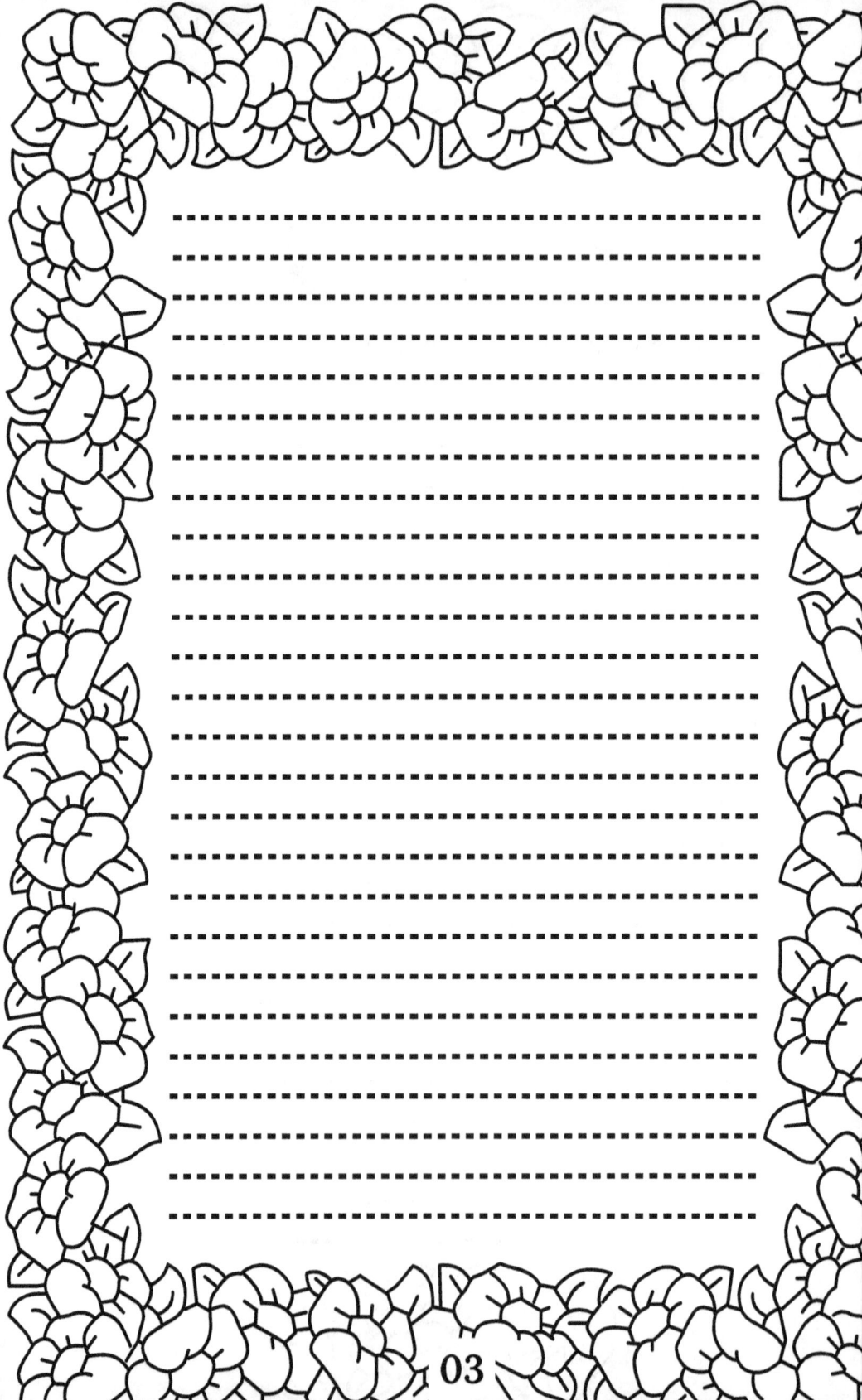

Day: 2

What do you love and appreciate about them?

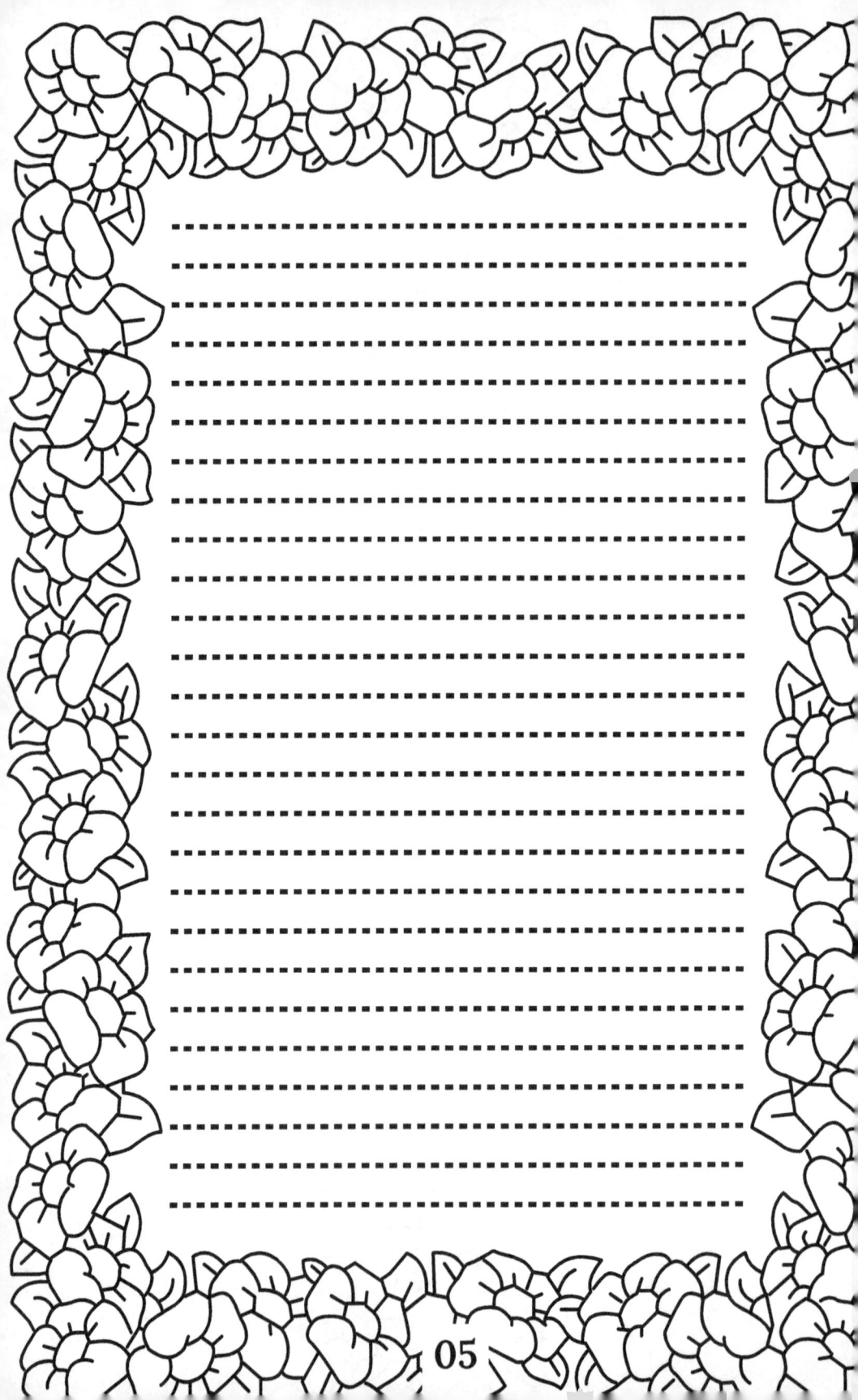

Day: 3

What is your favorite childhood memory about them?

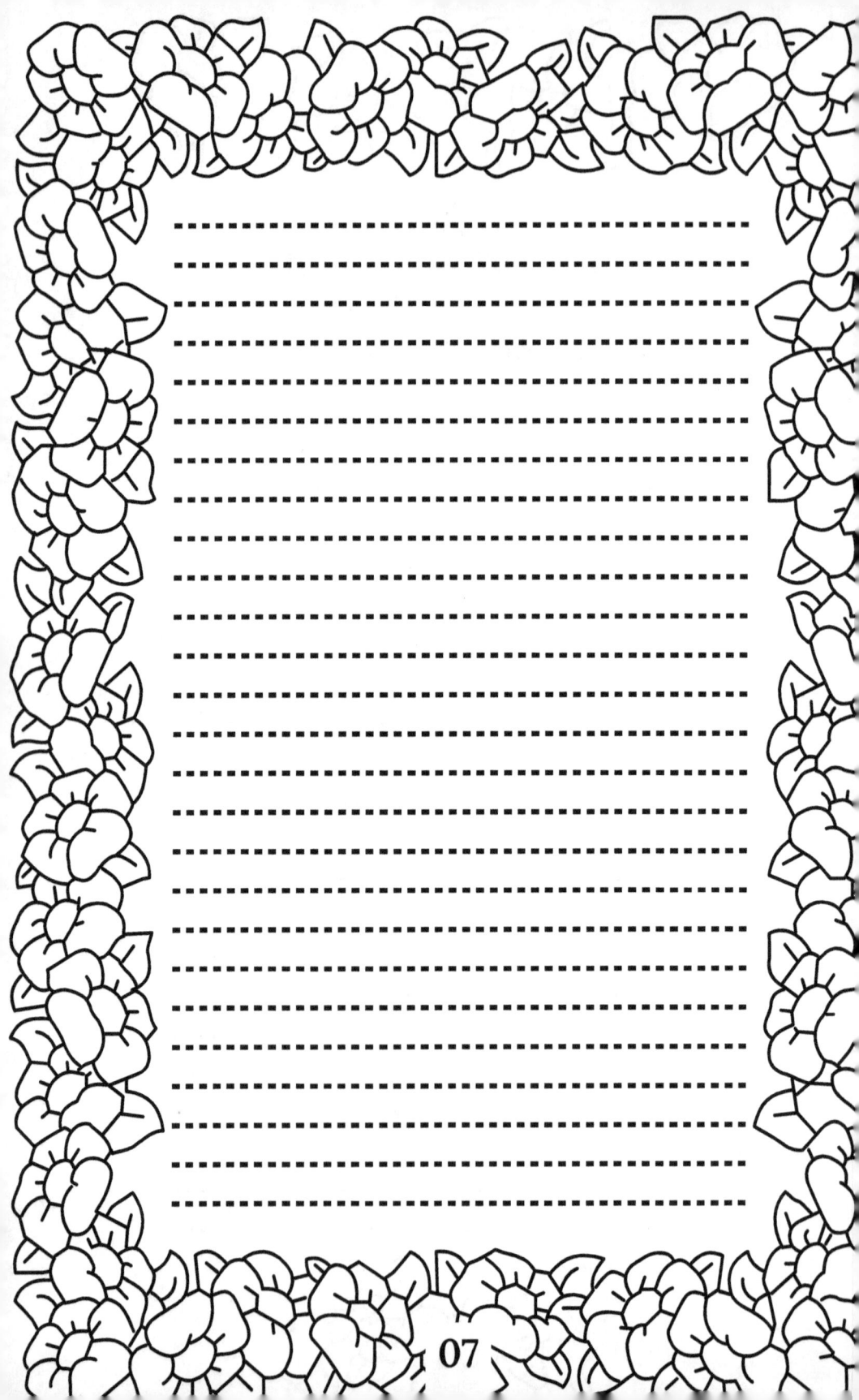

Day: 4

Describe a recent conflict with your sibling.

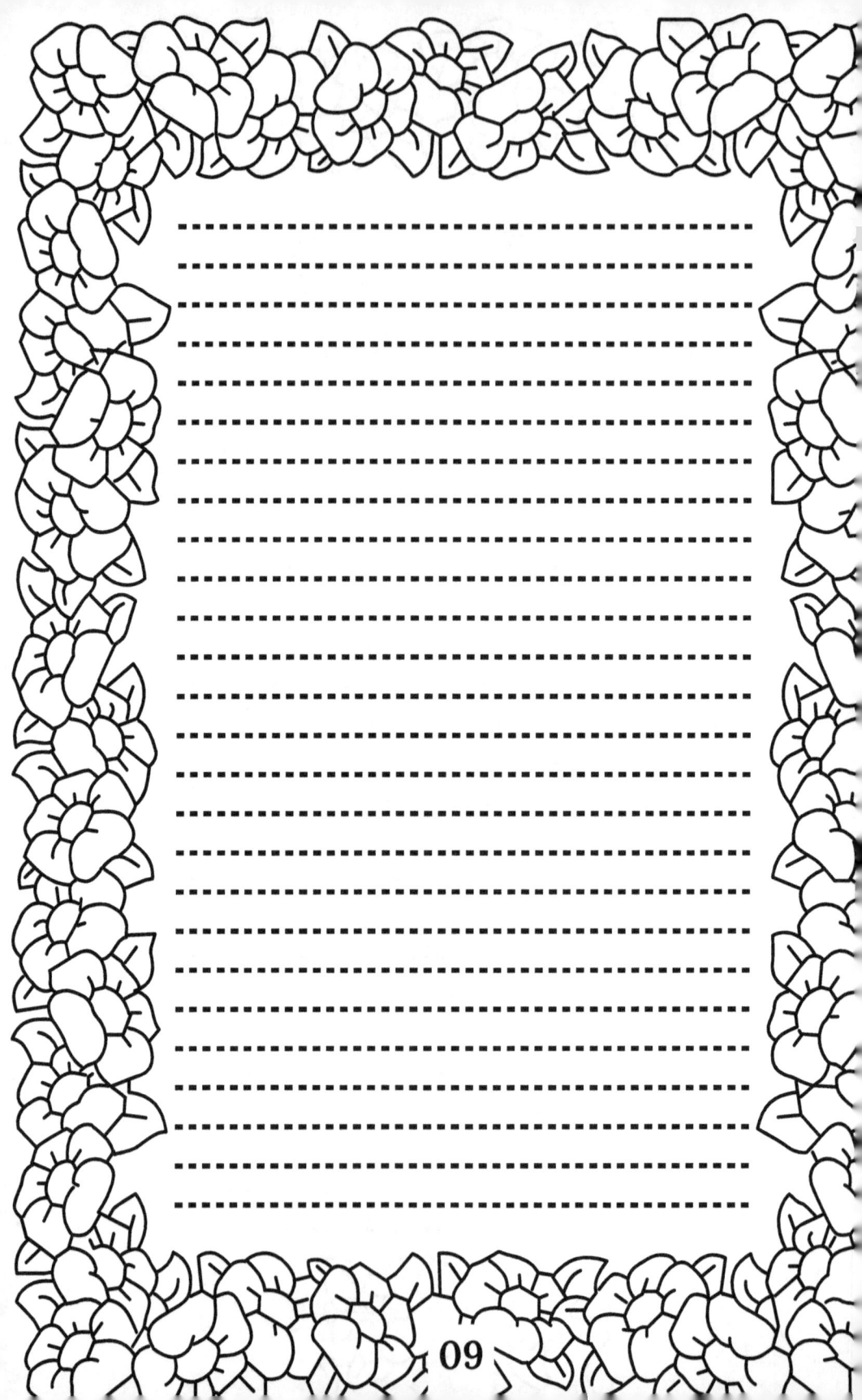

Day: 5

What emotion did it trigger after the conflict?

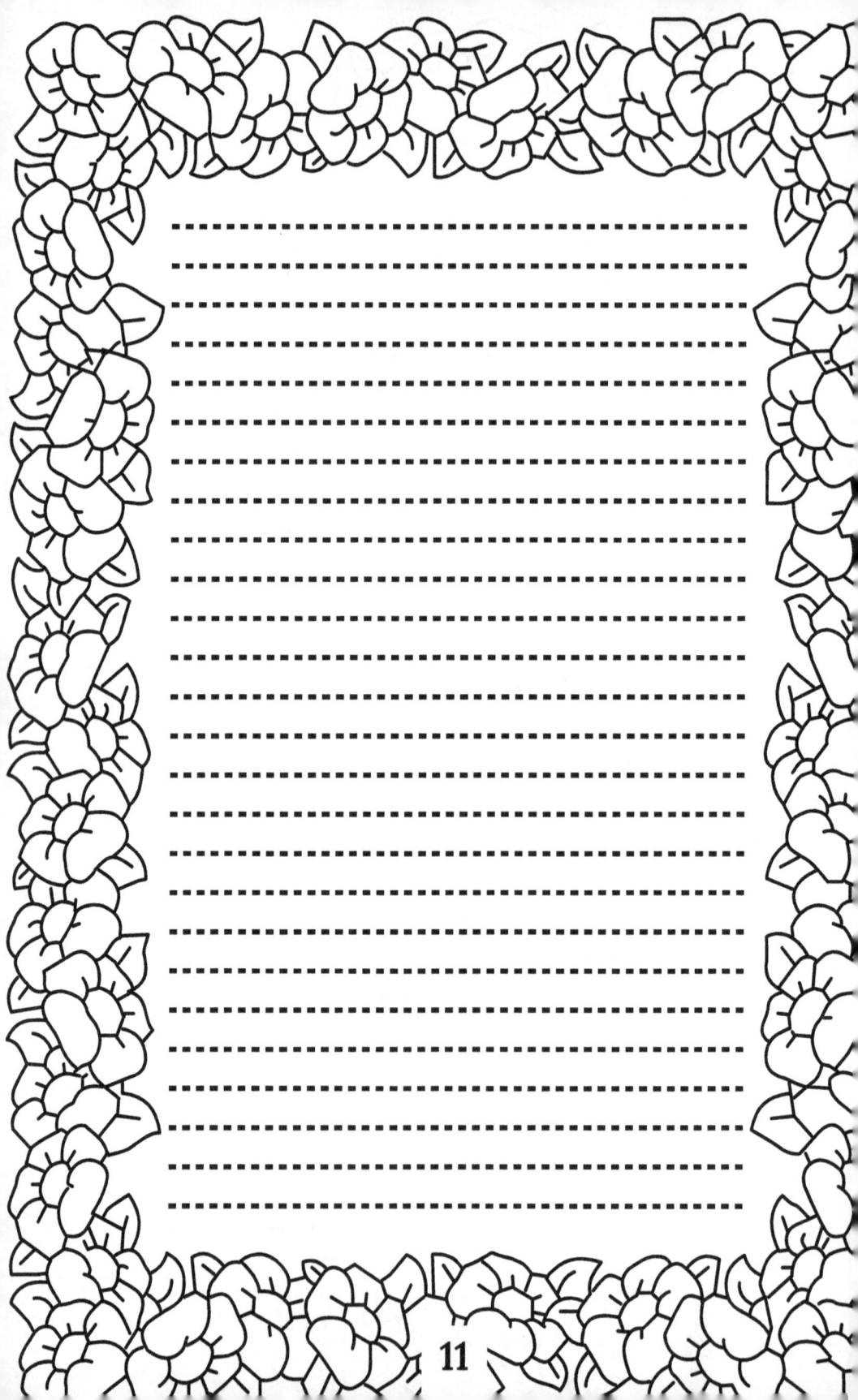

Day: 6

How did you respond?

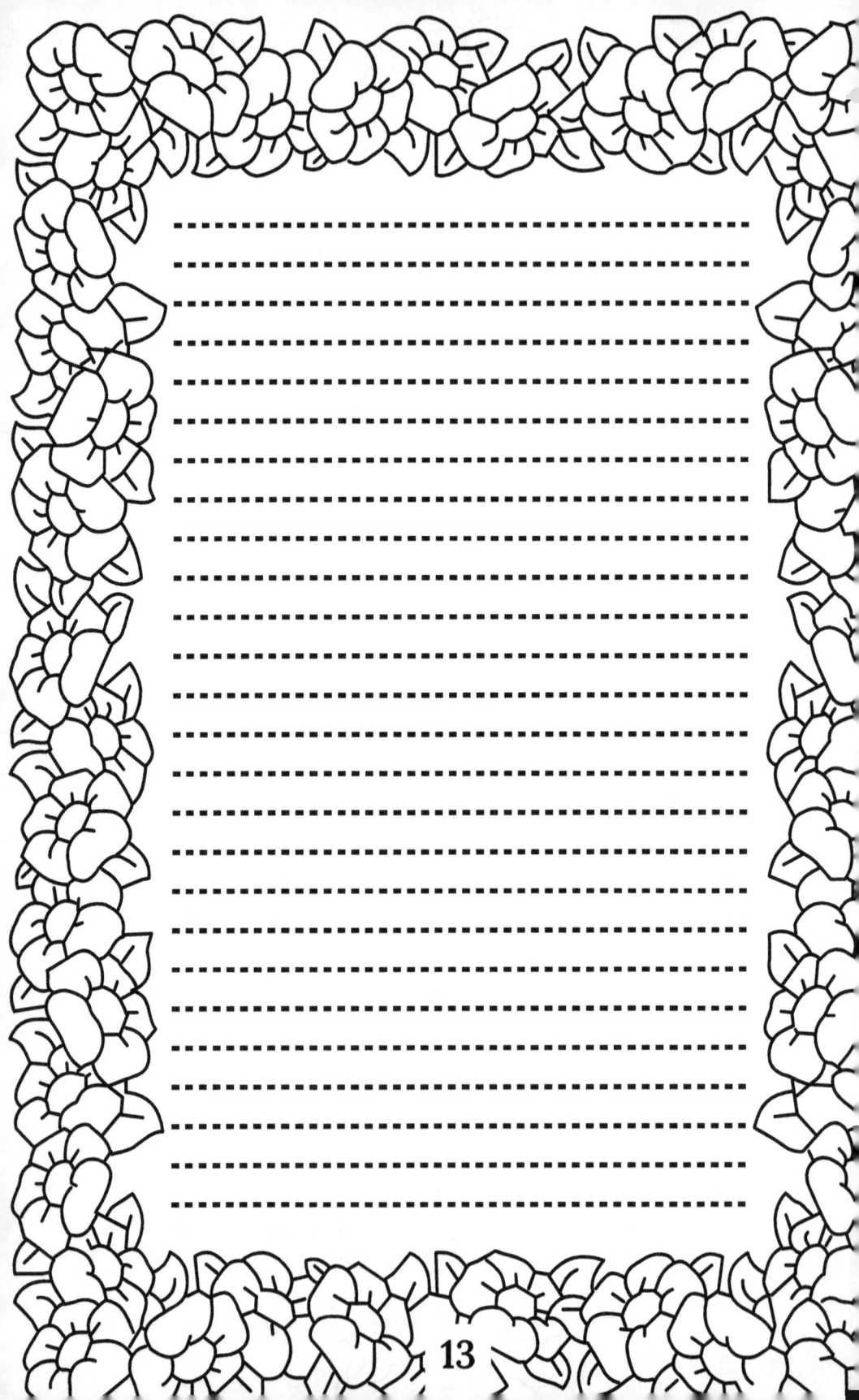

Day: 7

How did they respond?

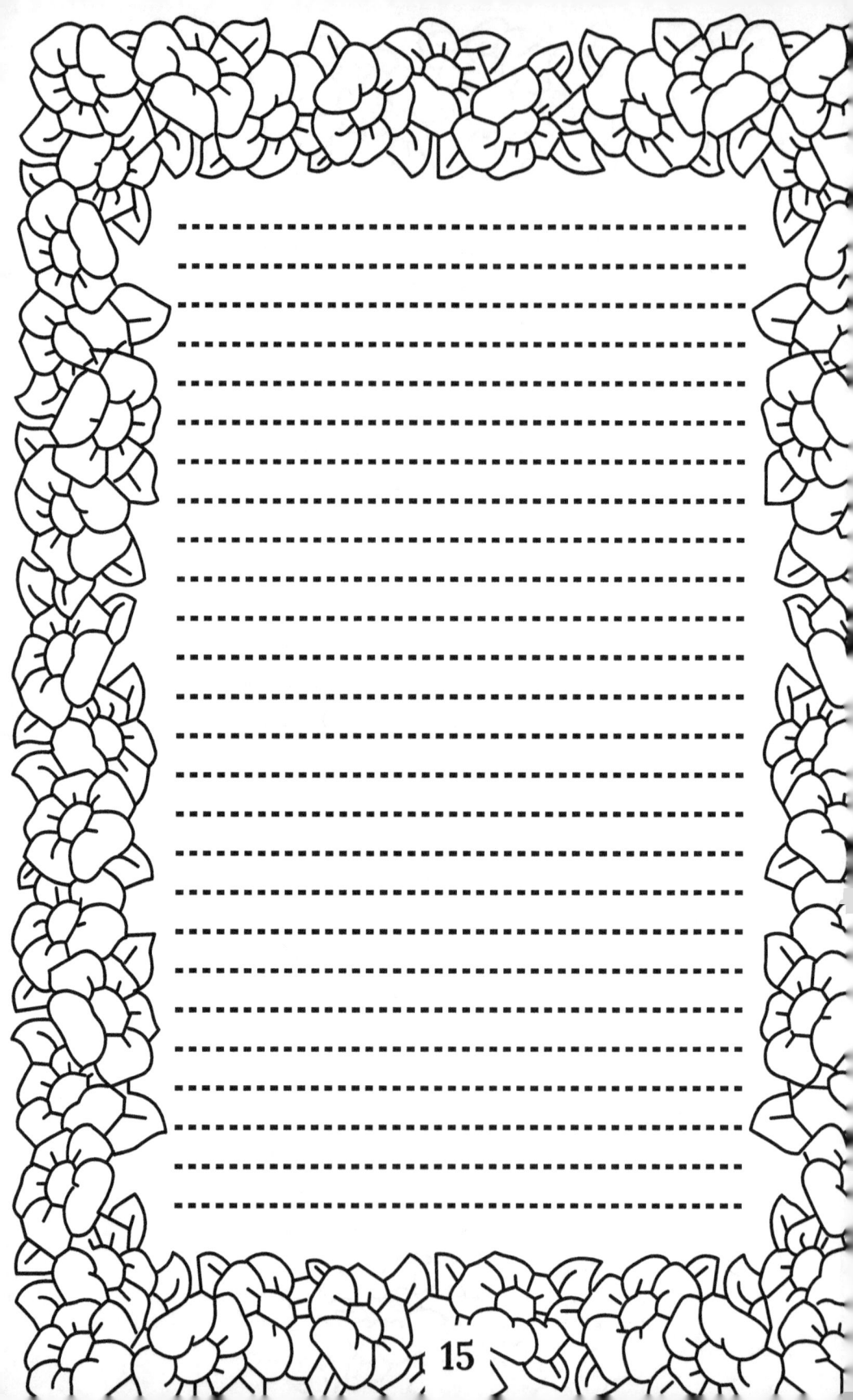

Day: 8

How do you typically respond after conflict?

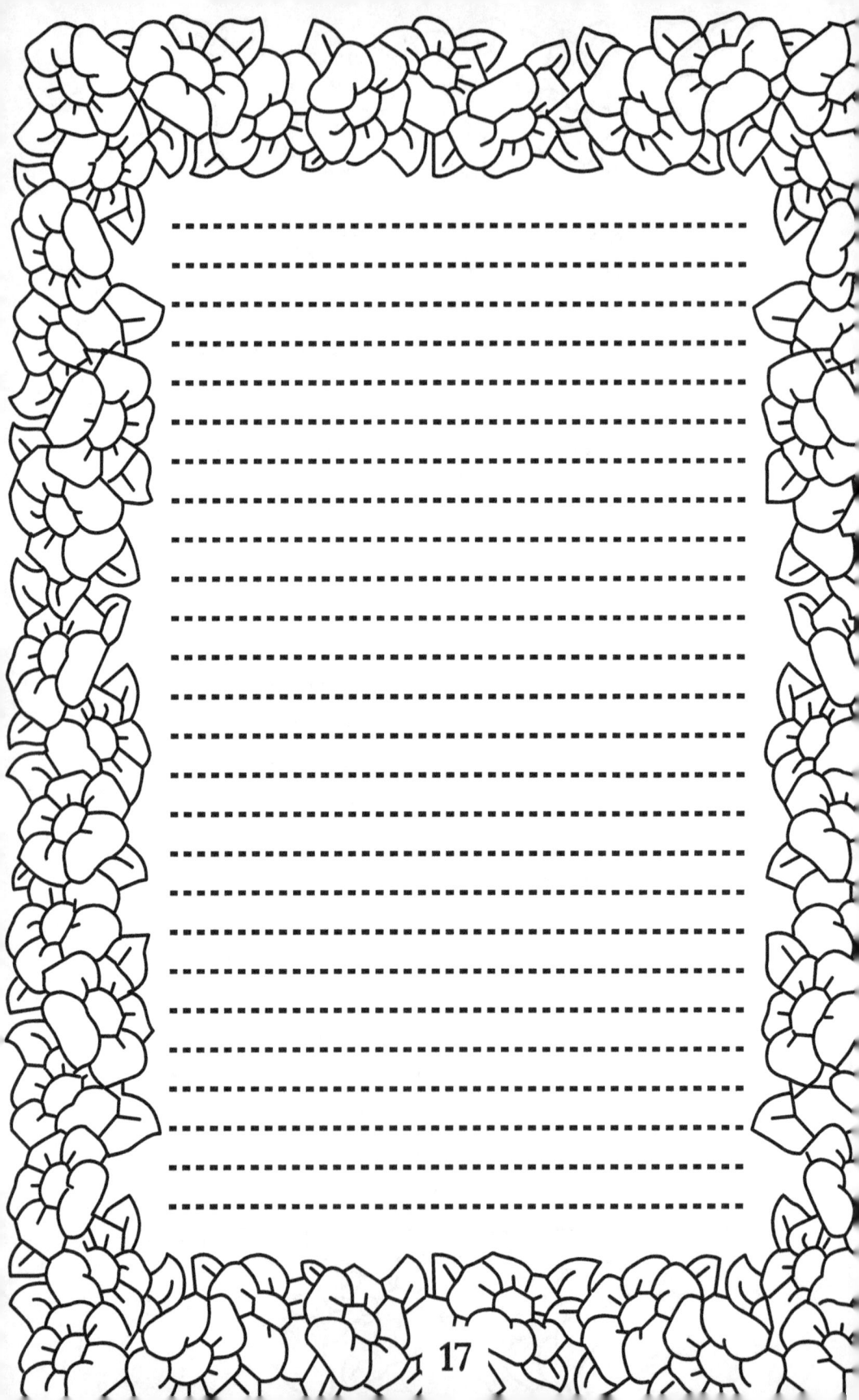

Day: 9

Is there a pattern that you notice during interactions?

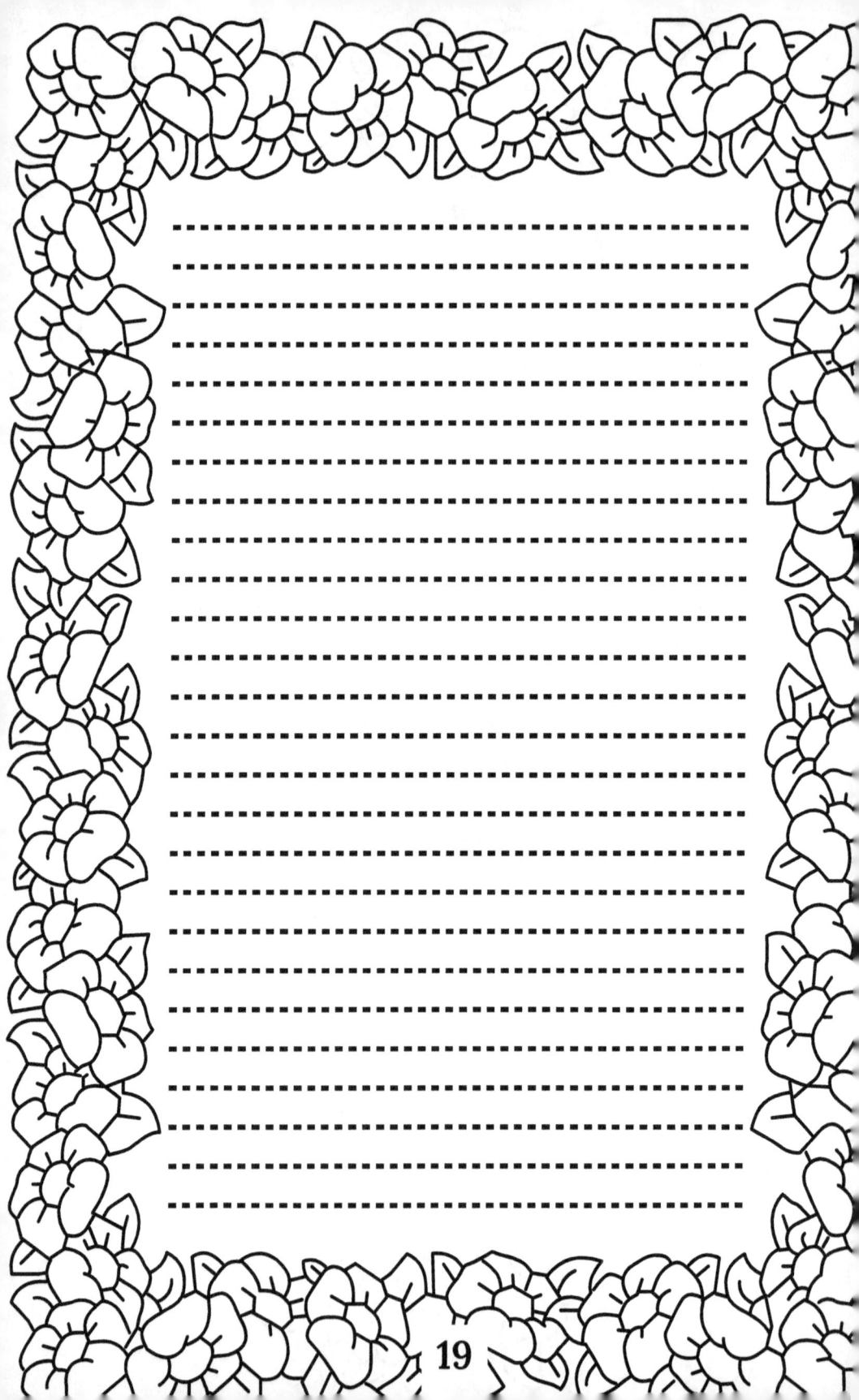

Day: 10

Reflect on your childhood roles in your family.

....
....
....
....
....
....
....
....
....
....
....
....
....
....
....
....
....
....
....
....
....

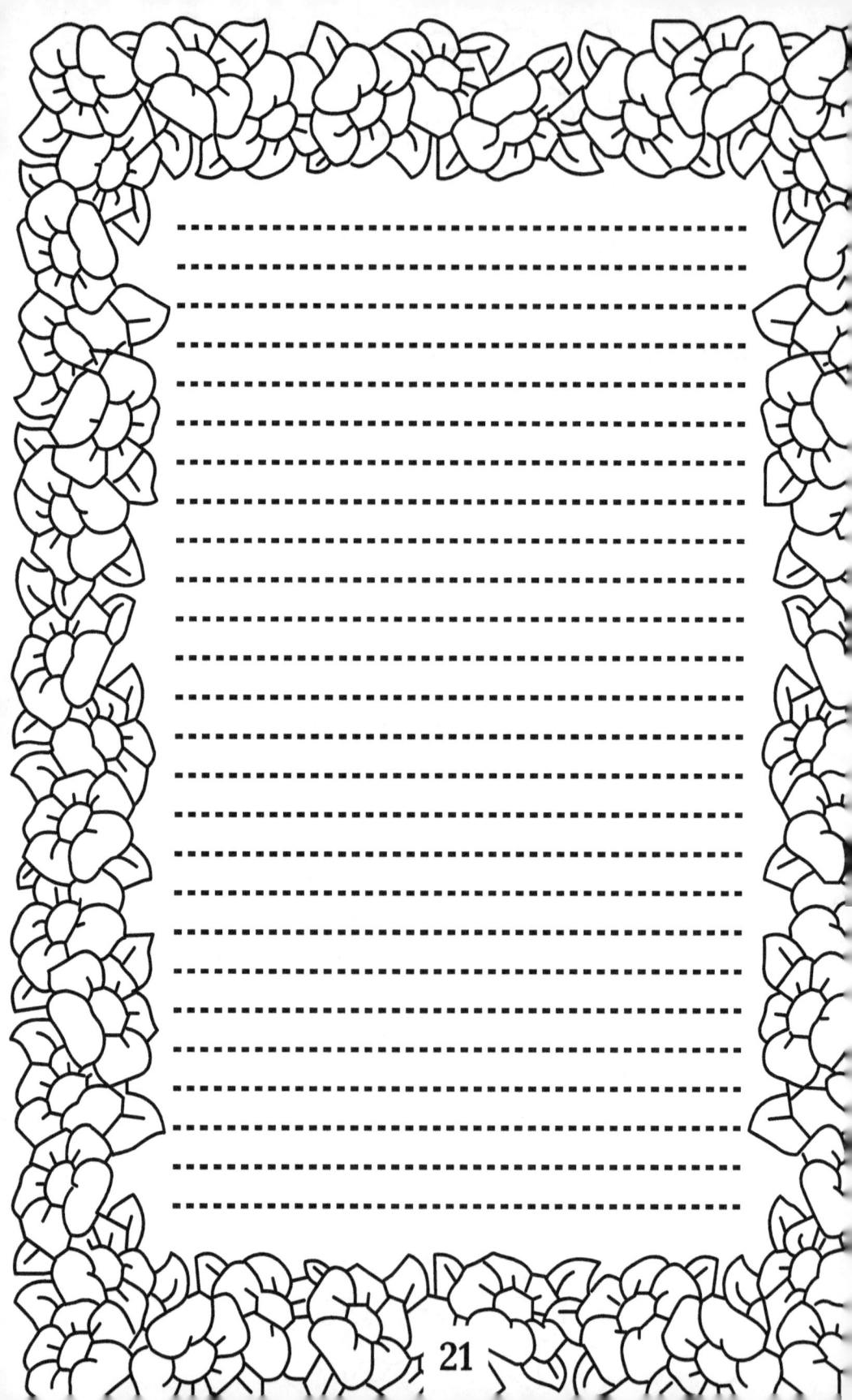

Day: 11

How does it affect your role(s) as an adult?.

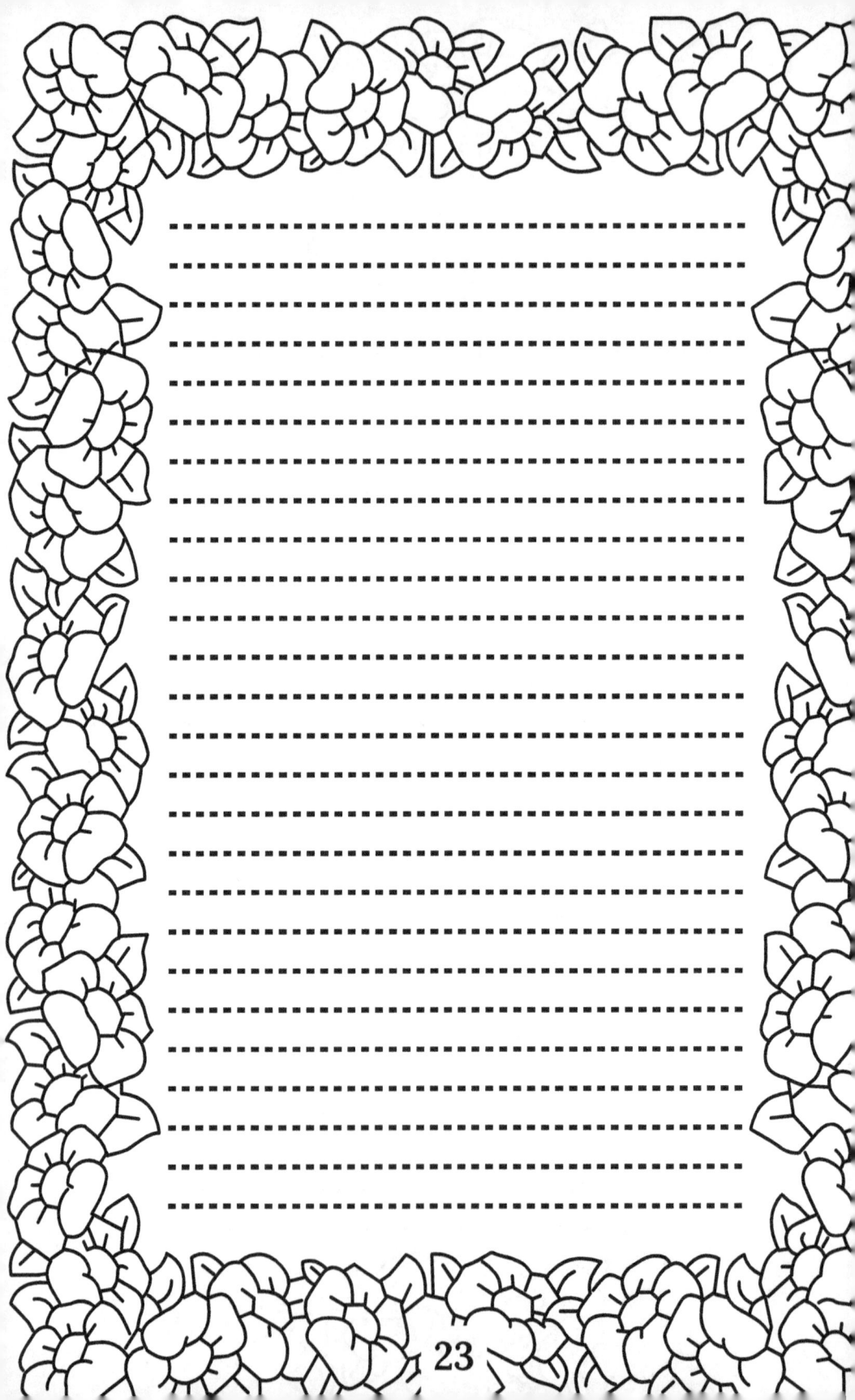

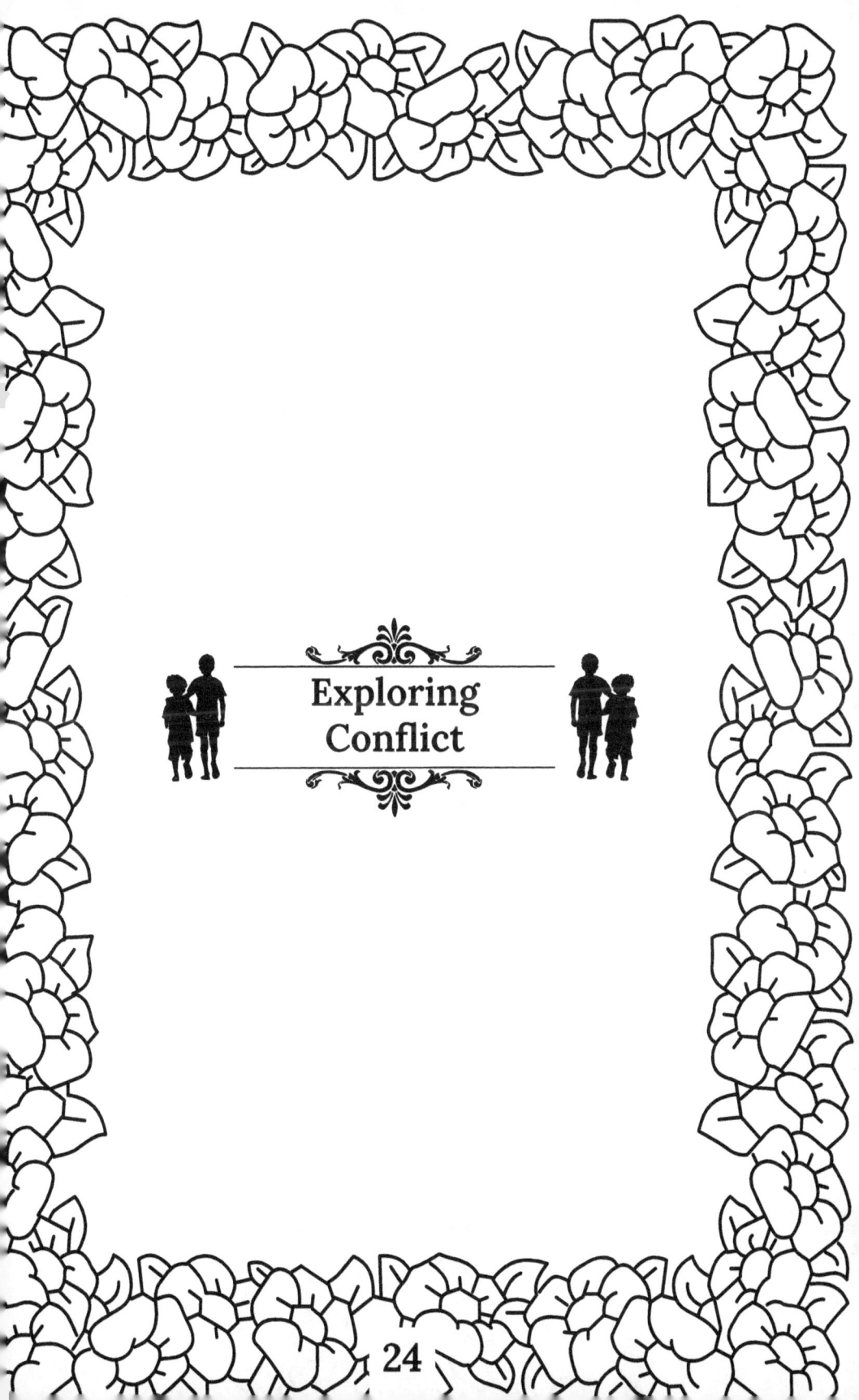

Exploring Conflict

Day: 12

How do you feel after a conflict is left unresolved?

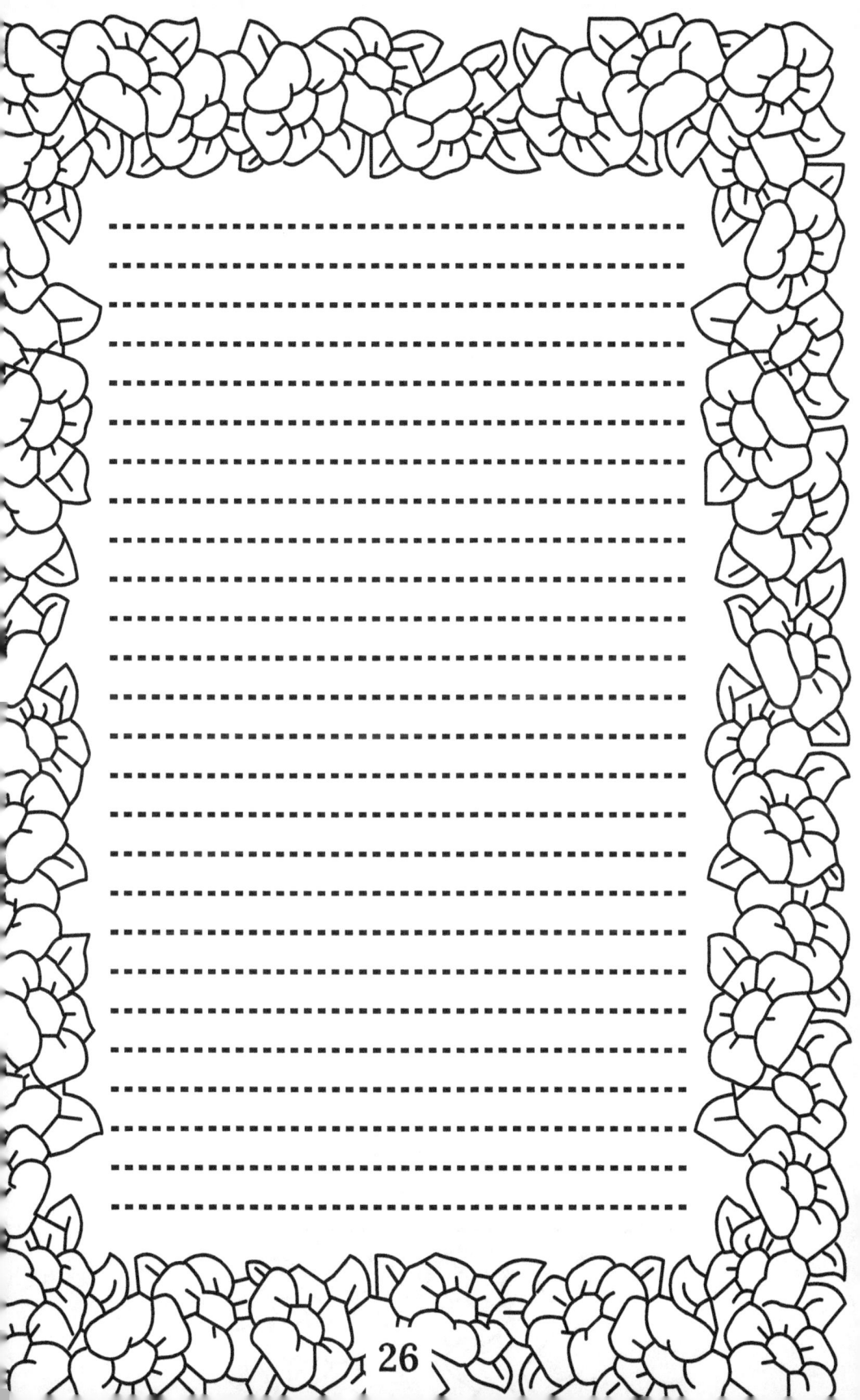

Day: 13

How do you feel after a conflict is resolved?

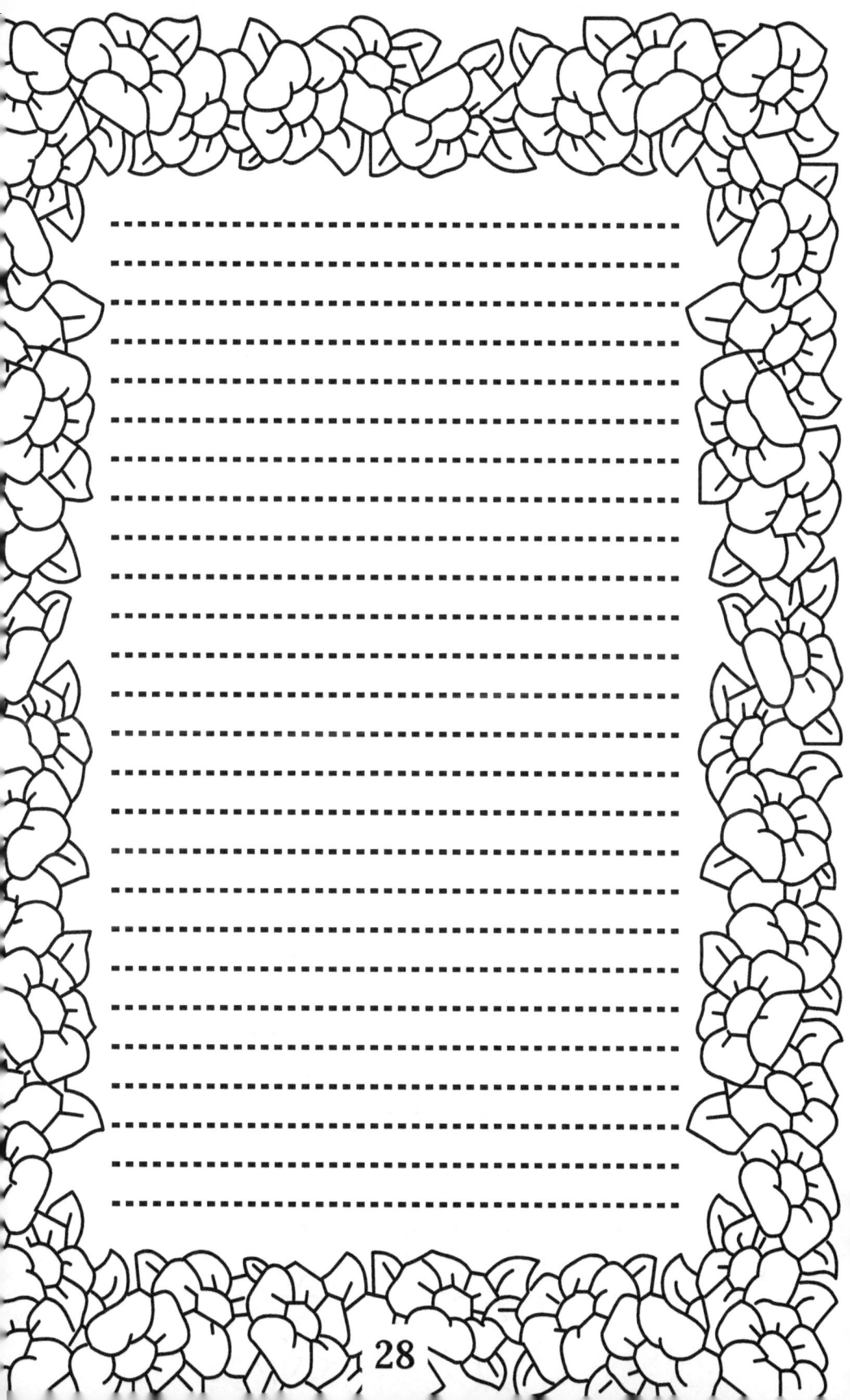

Day: 14

Reflect on an incident when you felt misunderstood by a sibling.

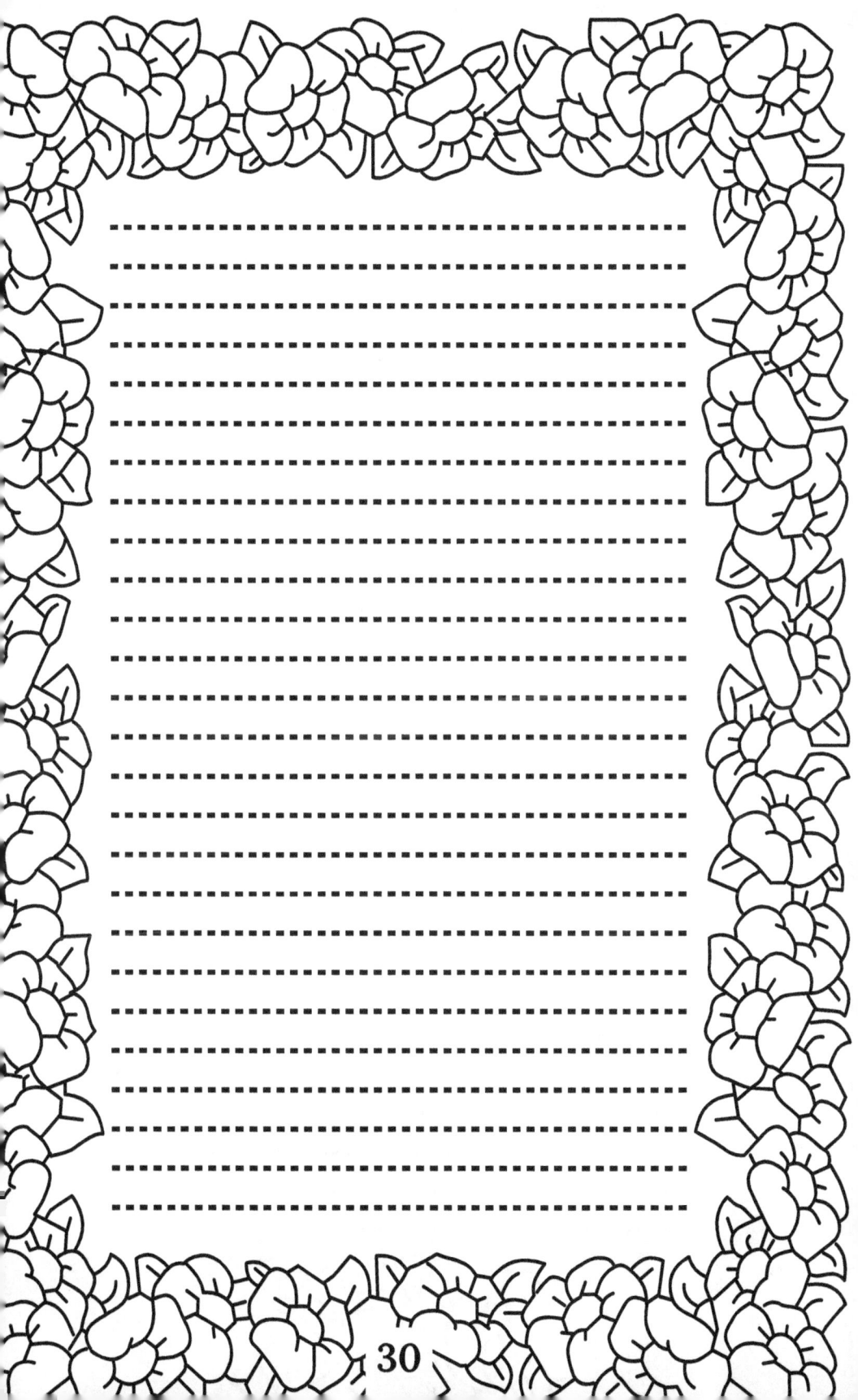

Day: 15

Describe an incident when you felt supported by your siblings.

....
....
....
....
....
....
....
....
....
....
....
....
....
....
....
....
....
....
....

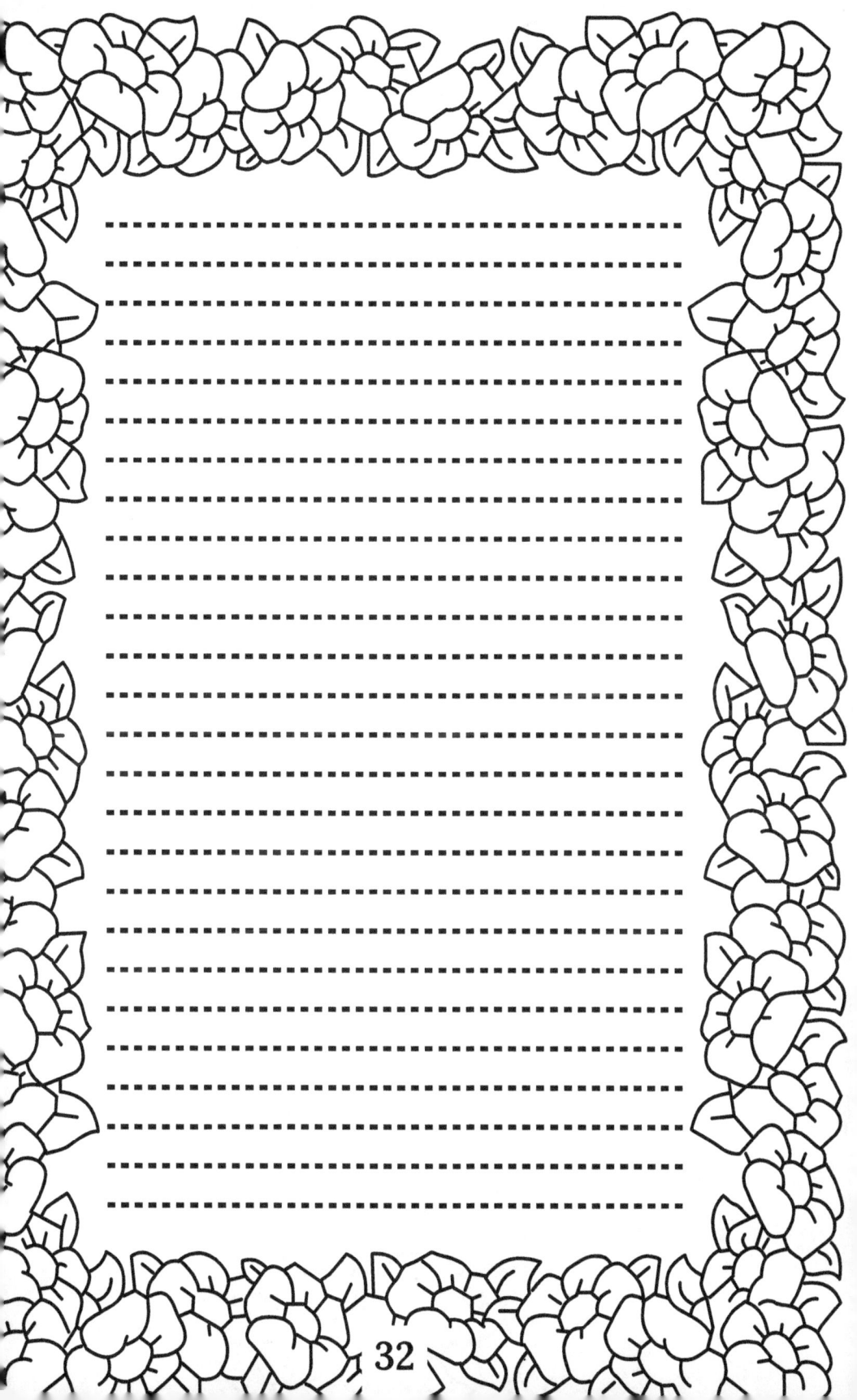

Day: 16

How do you think your siblings view you through their eyes?

....
....
....
....
....
....
....
....
....
....
....
....
....
....
....
....
....
....
....
....

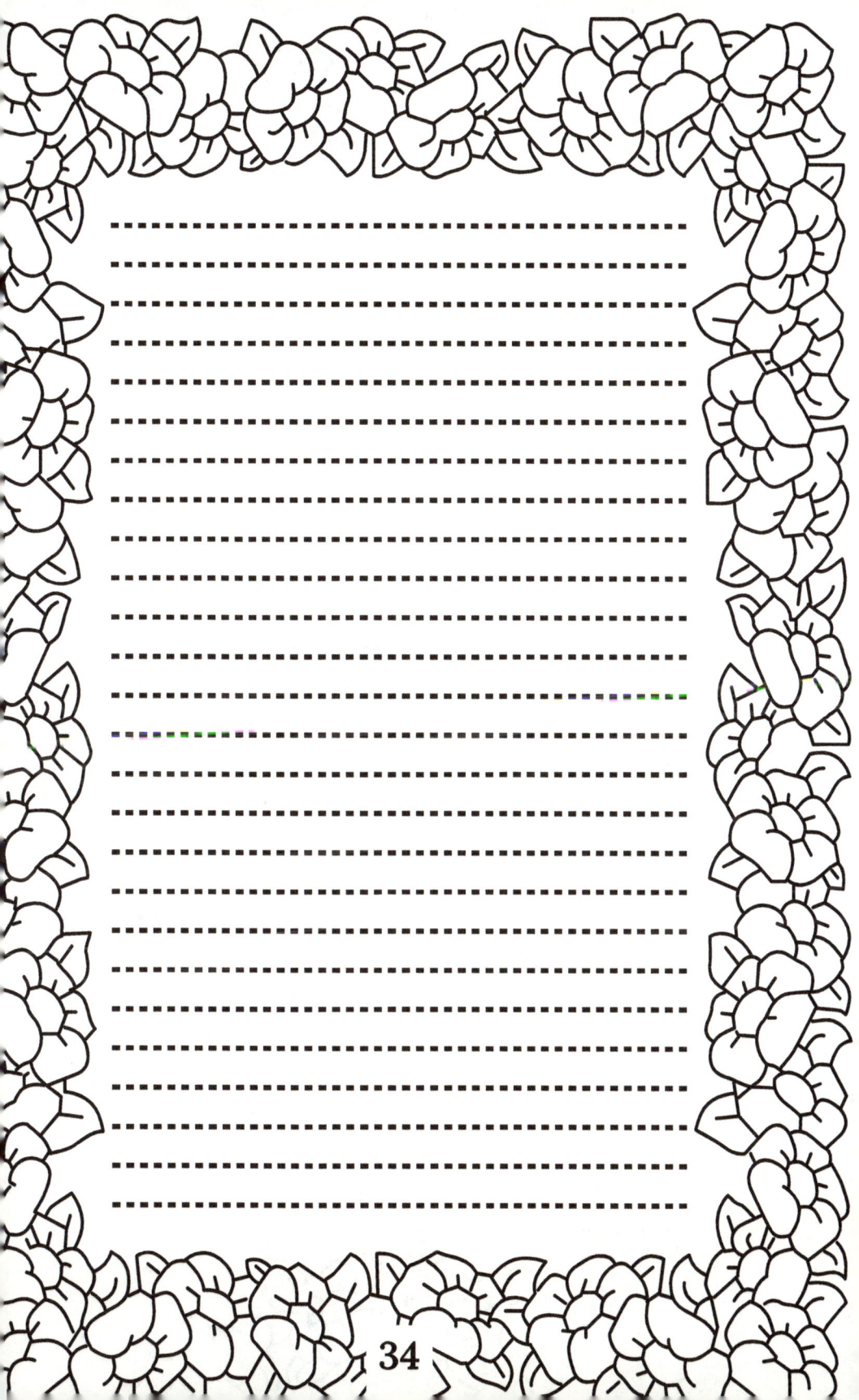

Day: 17

Do you agree or disagree with their thoughts of you? Why or why not?

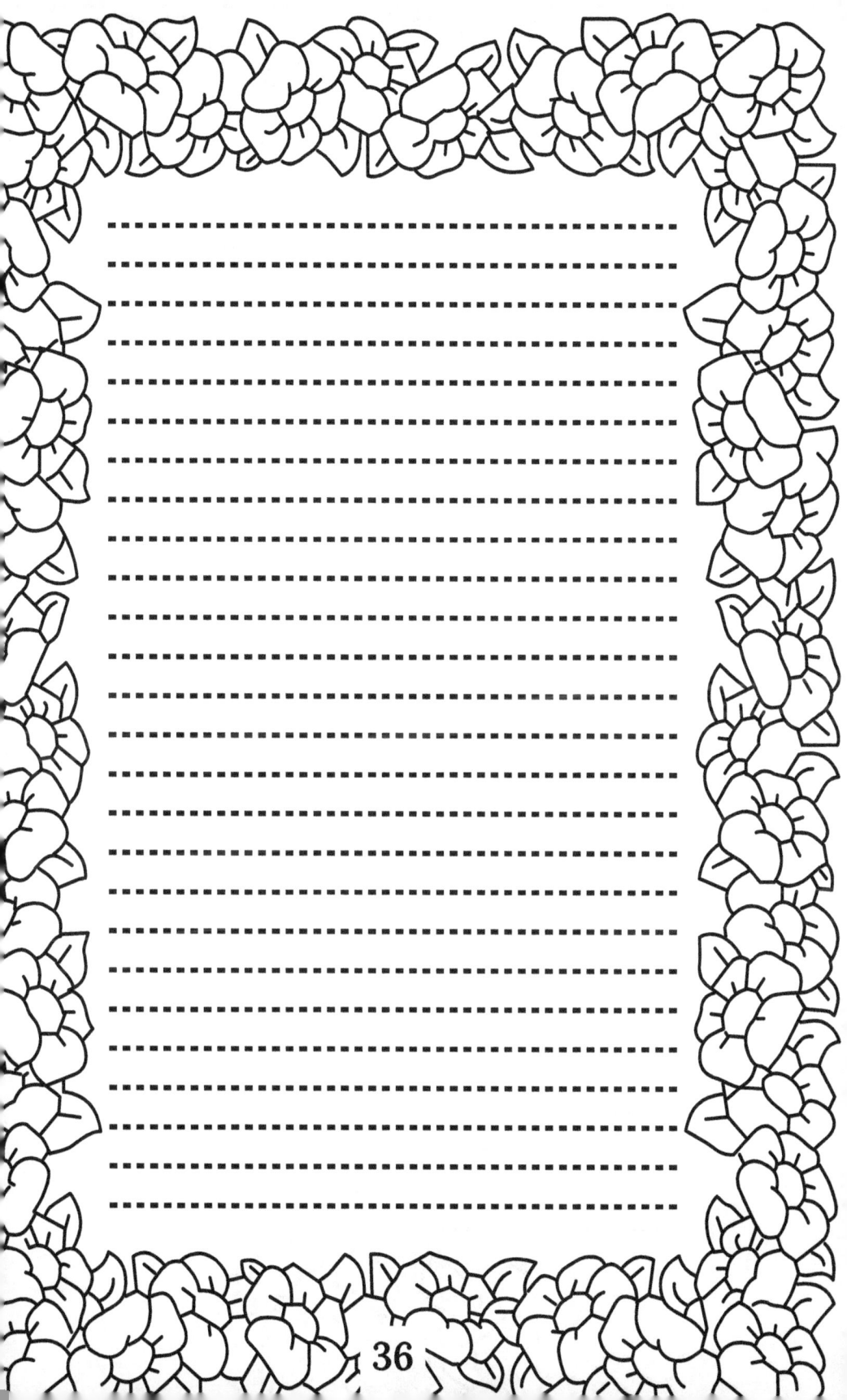

Day: 18

Write about a significant conflict from your past.

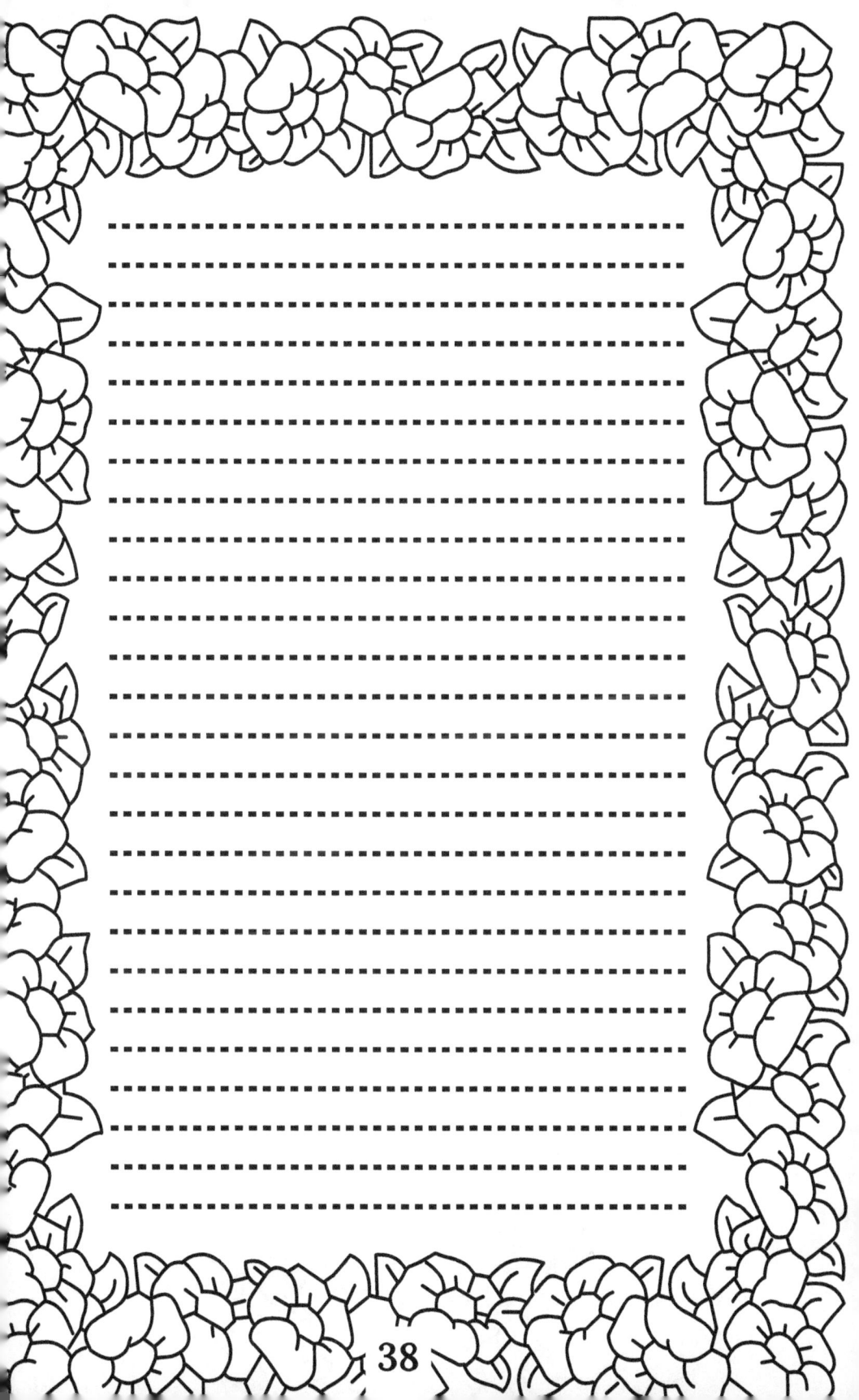

Day: 19

What do you believe that you could have done differently during that incident?

....
....
....
....
....
....
....
....
....
....
....
....
....
....
....
....
....
....

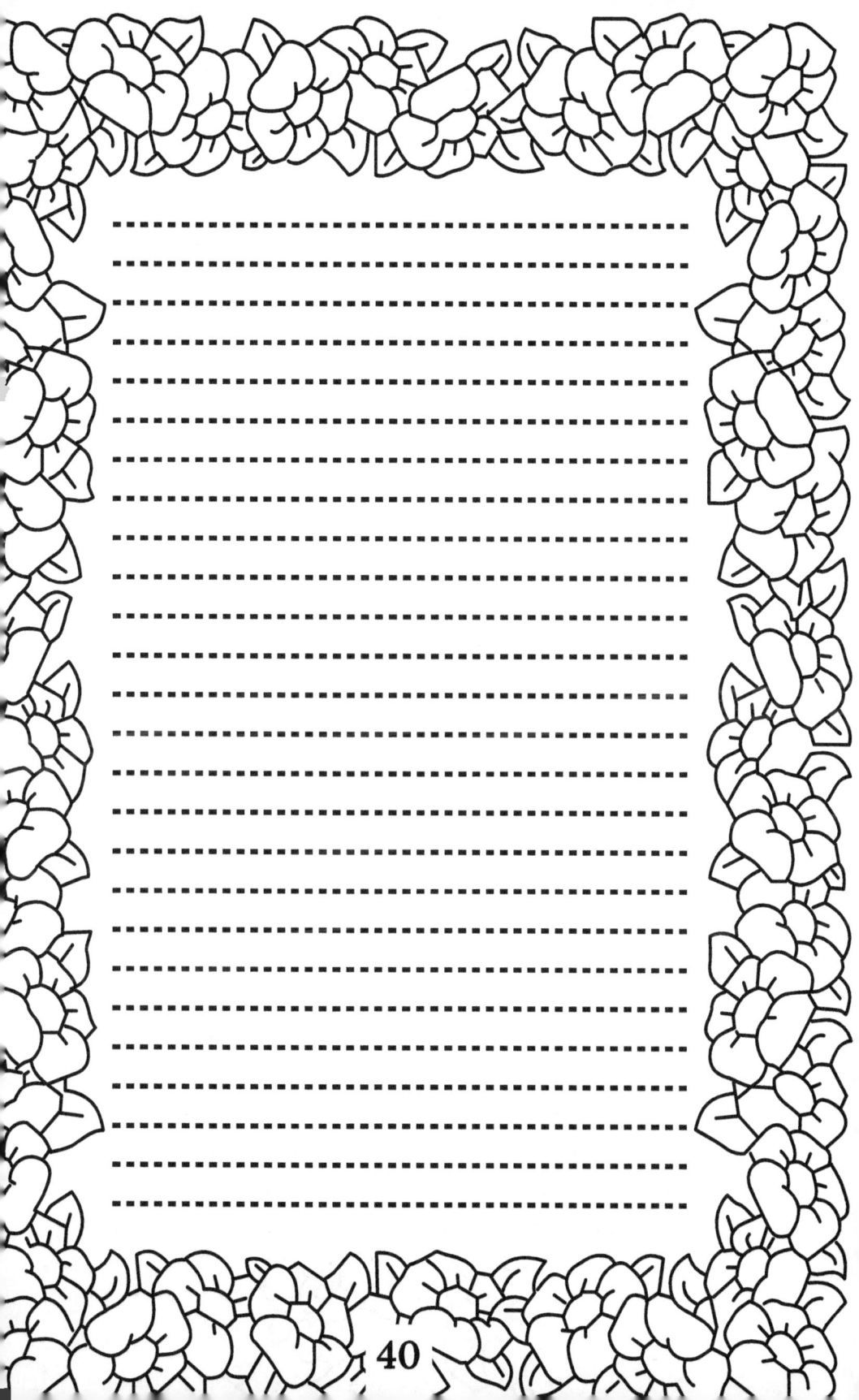

Day: 20

What triggers you during your conflicts with your siblings?

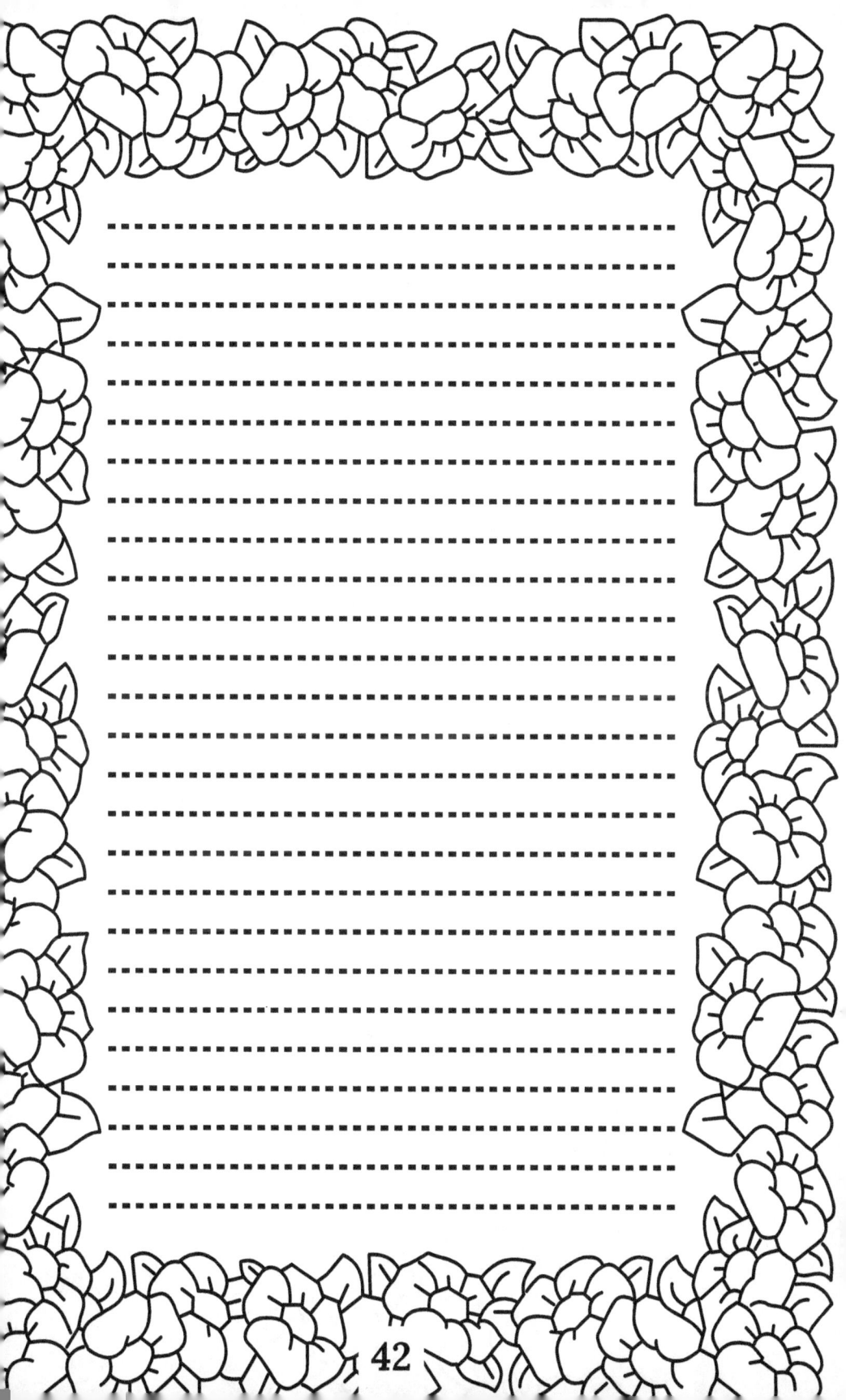

Day: 21

Are your siblings aware of your triggers? If they are not aware, why not?

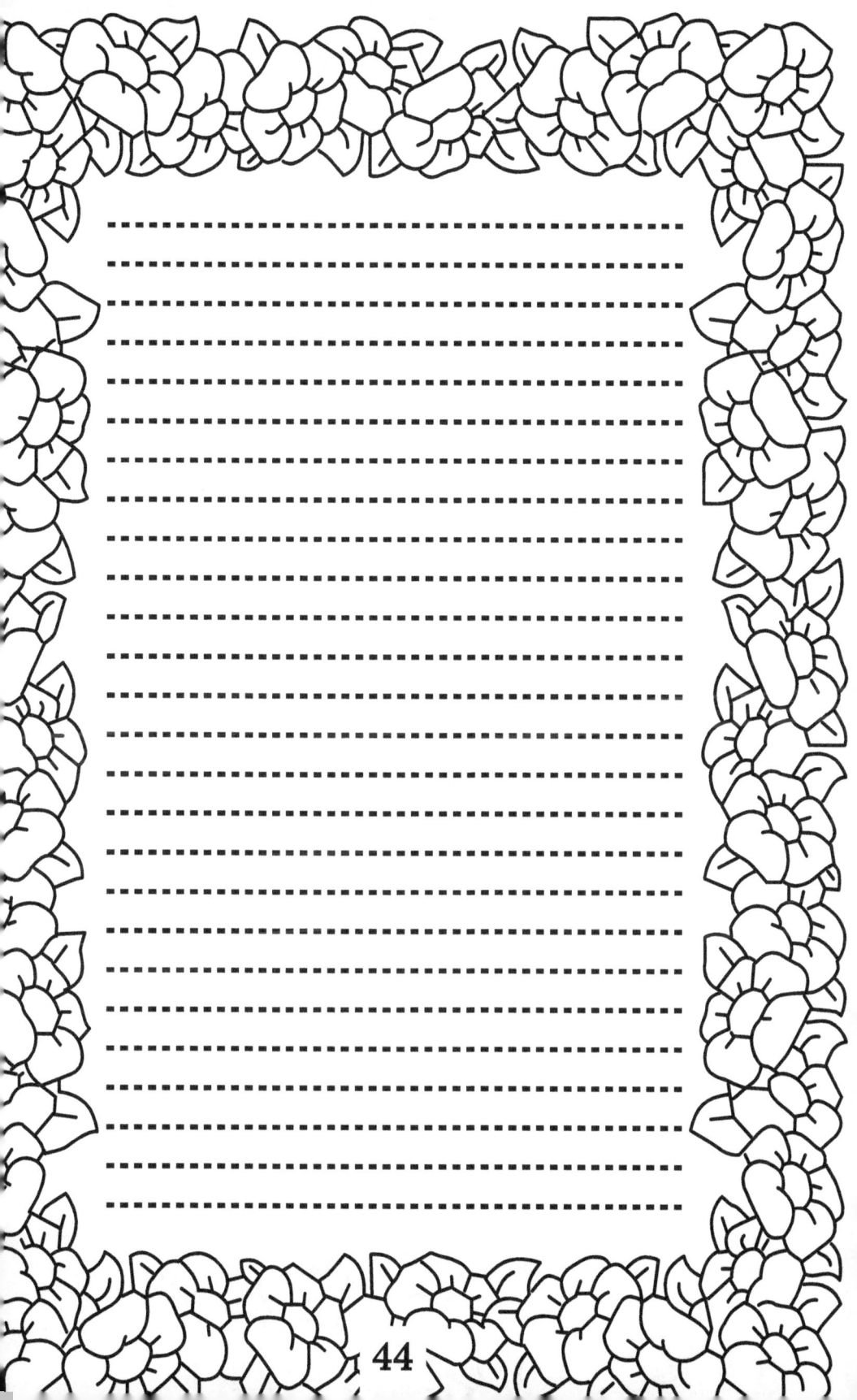

Day: 22

How do they respond to you when you are triggered?

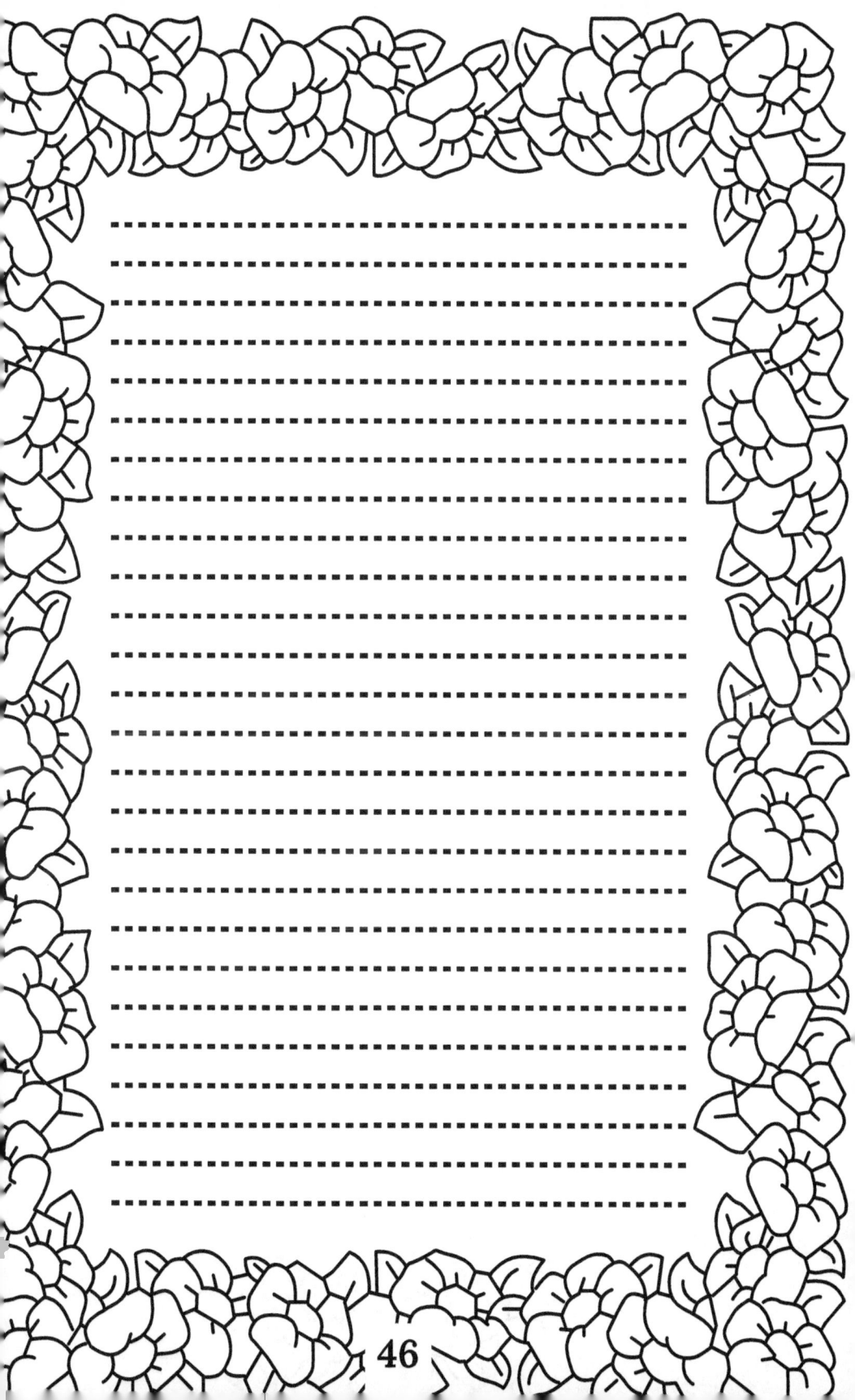

Emotional
Impact

Day: 23

Write a letter to your sibling expressing your feelings. You can choose to mail it or not.

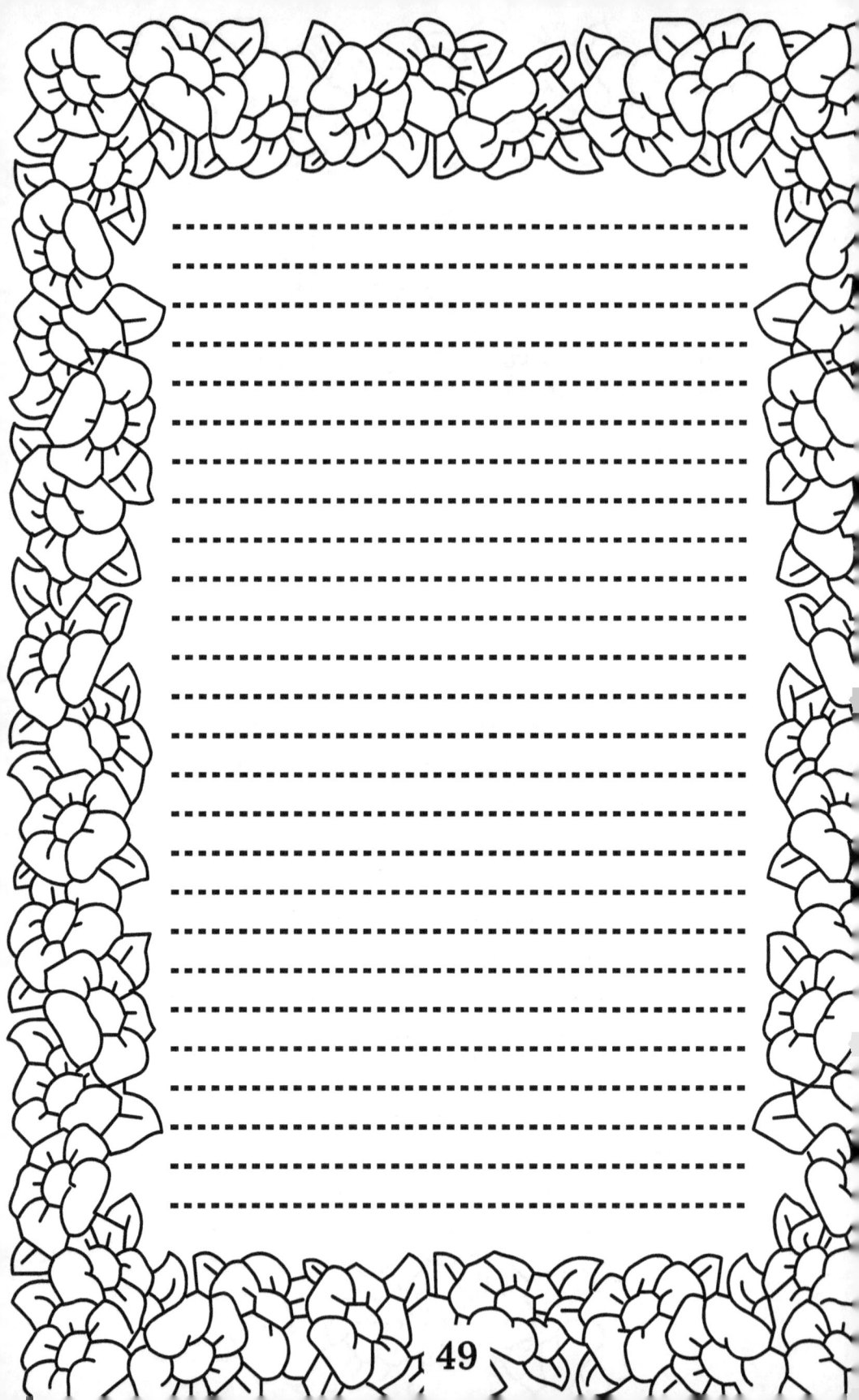

Day: 24

What steps can you take to heal your relationship with a specific sibling?

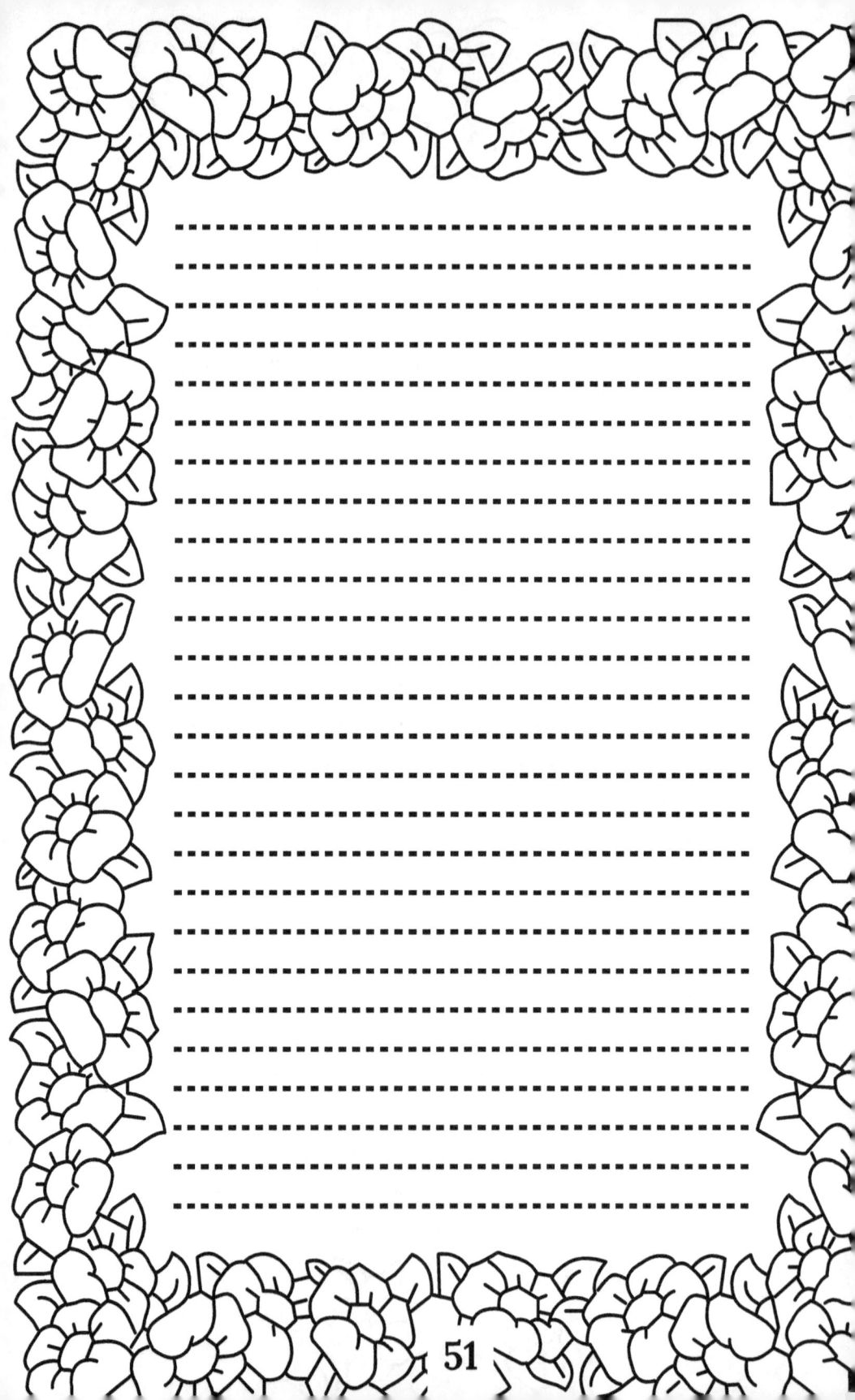

Day: 25

What does forgiveness mean to you in the context of your sibling relationship?

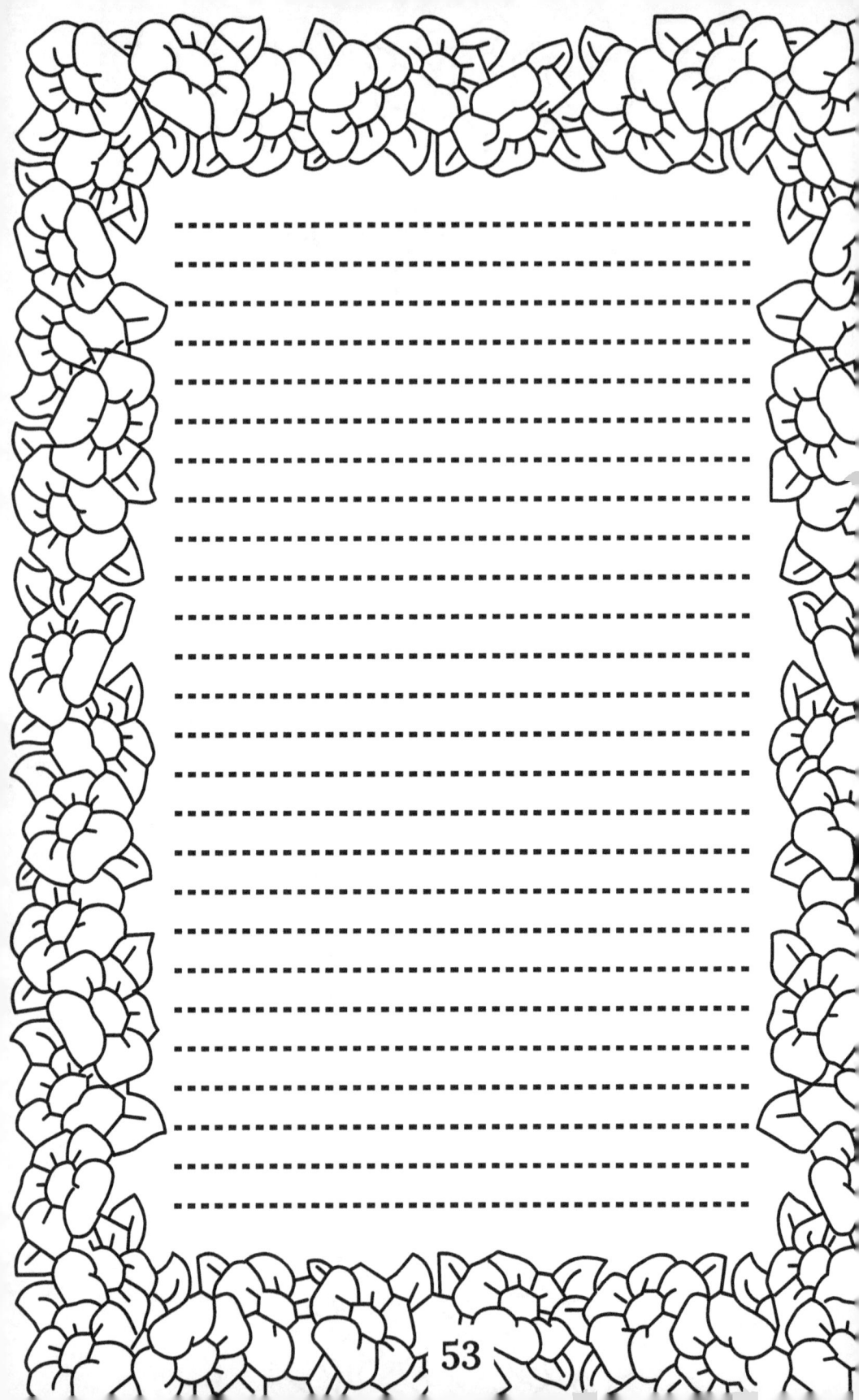

Day: 26

How can you cultivate empathy towards your siblings during conflicts?

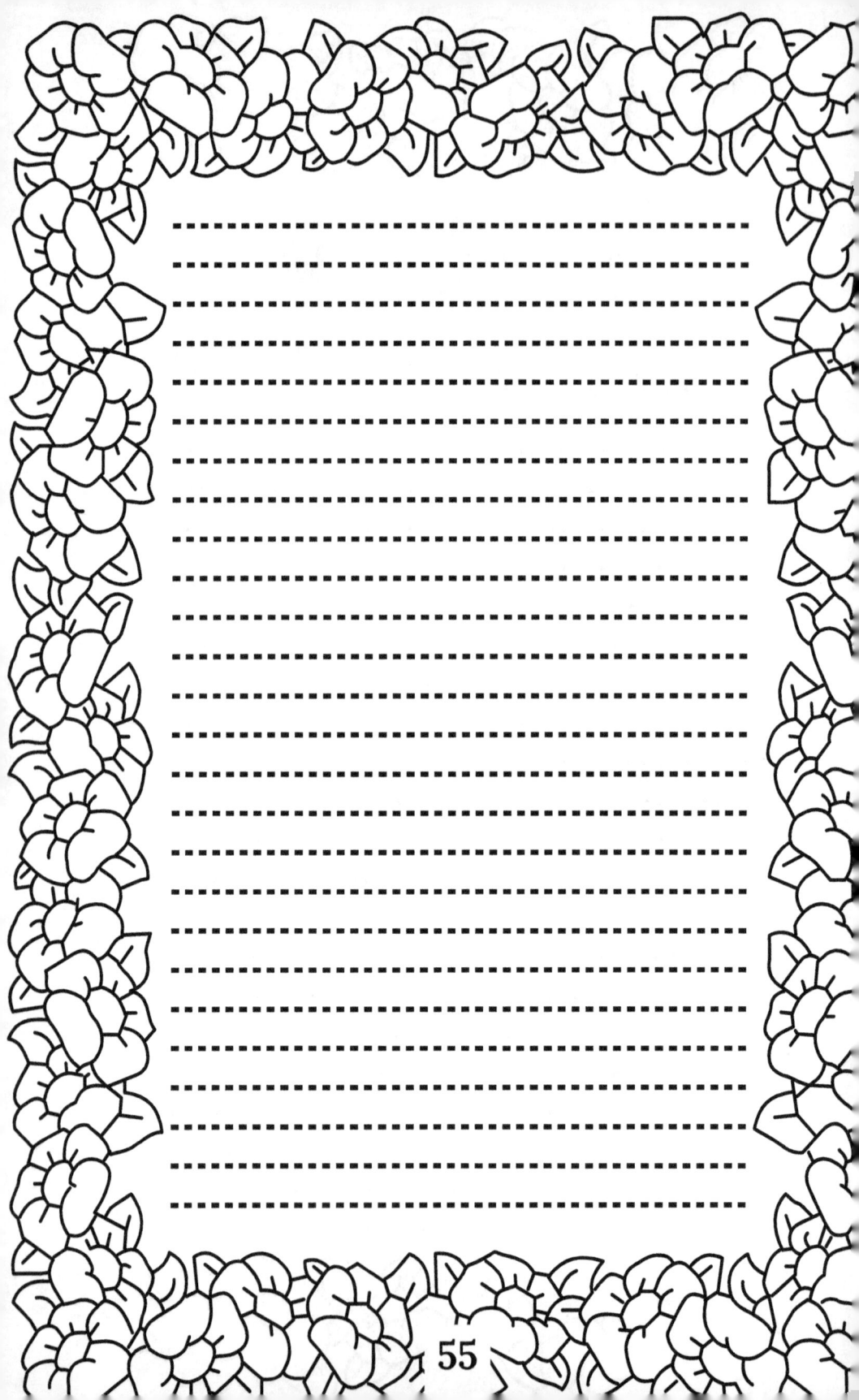

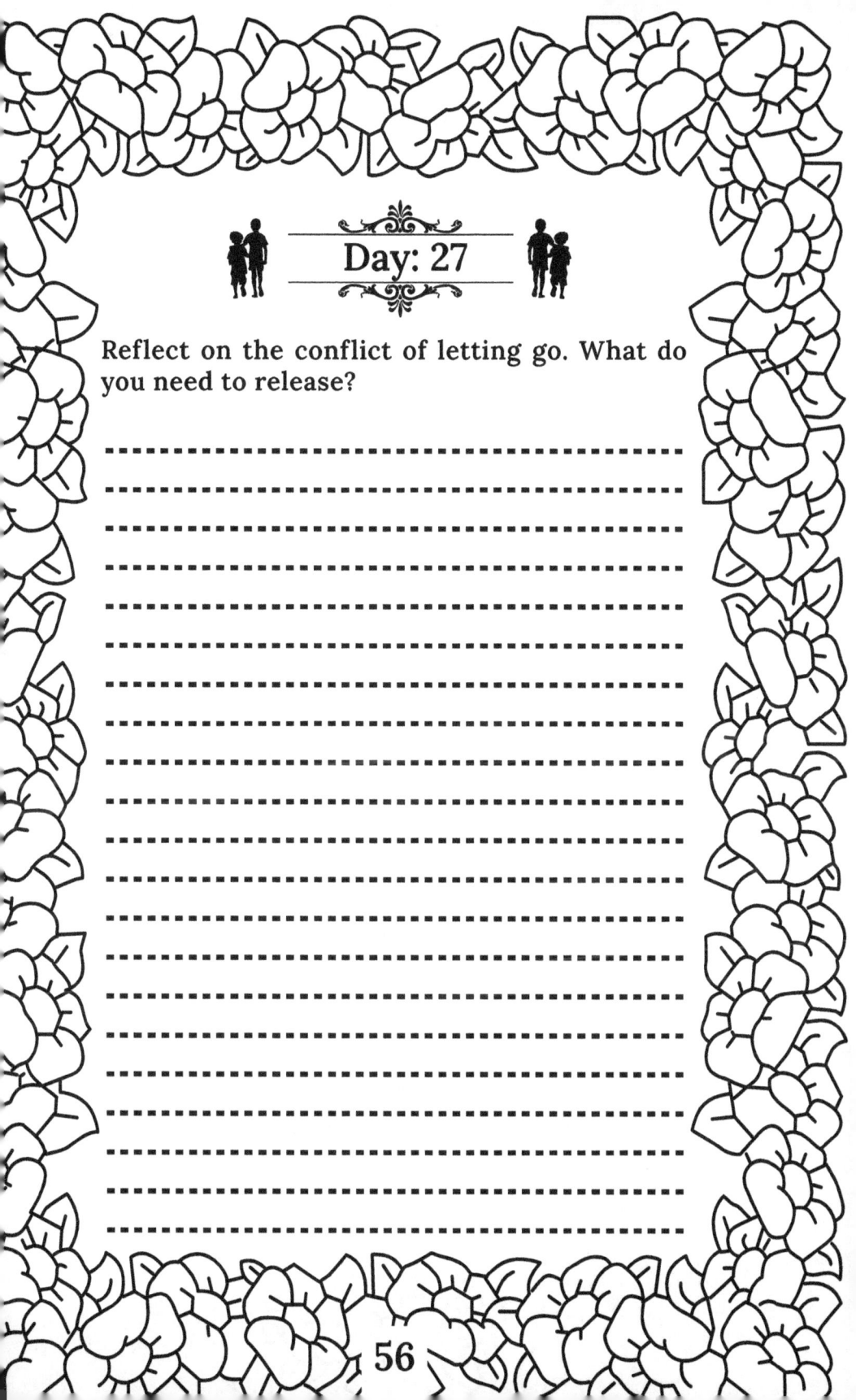

Day: 27

Reflect on the conflict of letting go. What do you need to release?

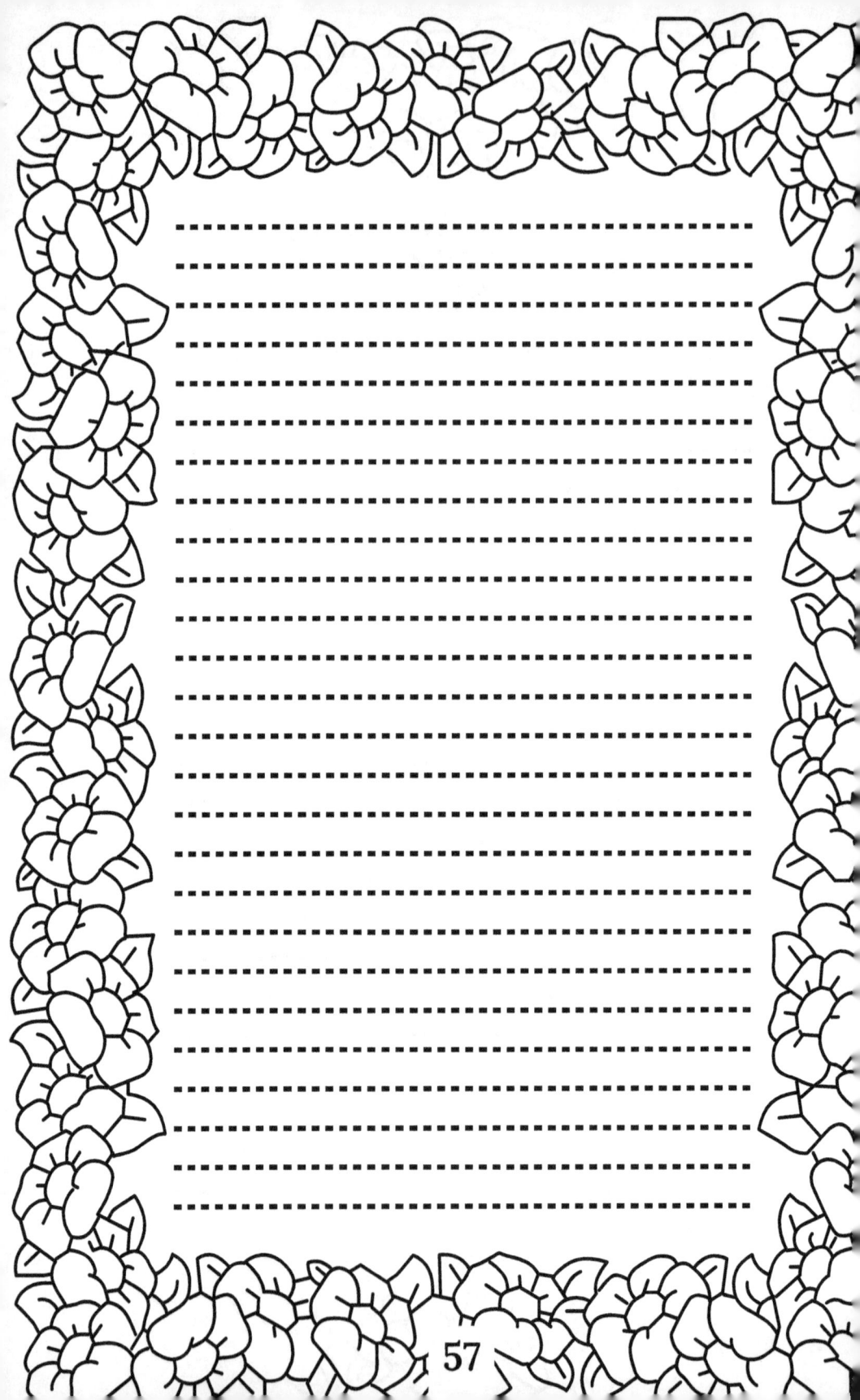

Day: 28

What self care practices can you implement to support your emotional health?

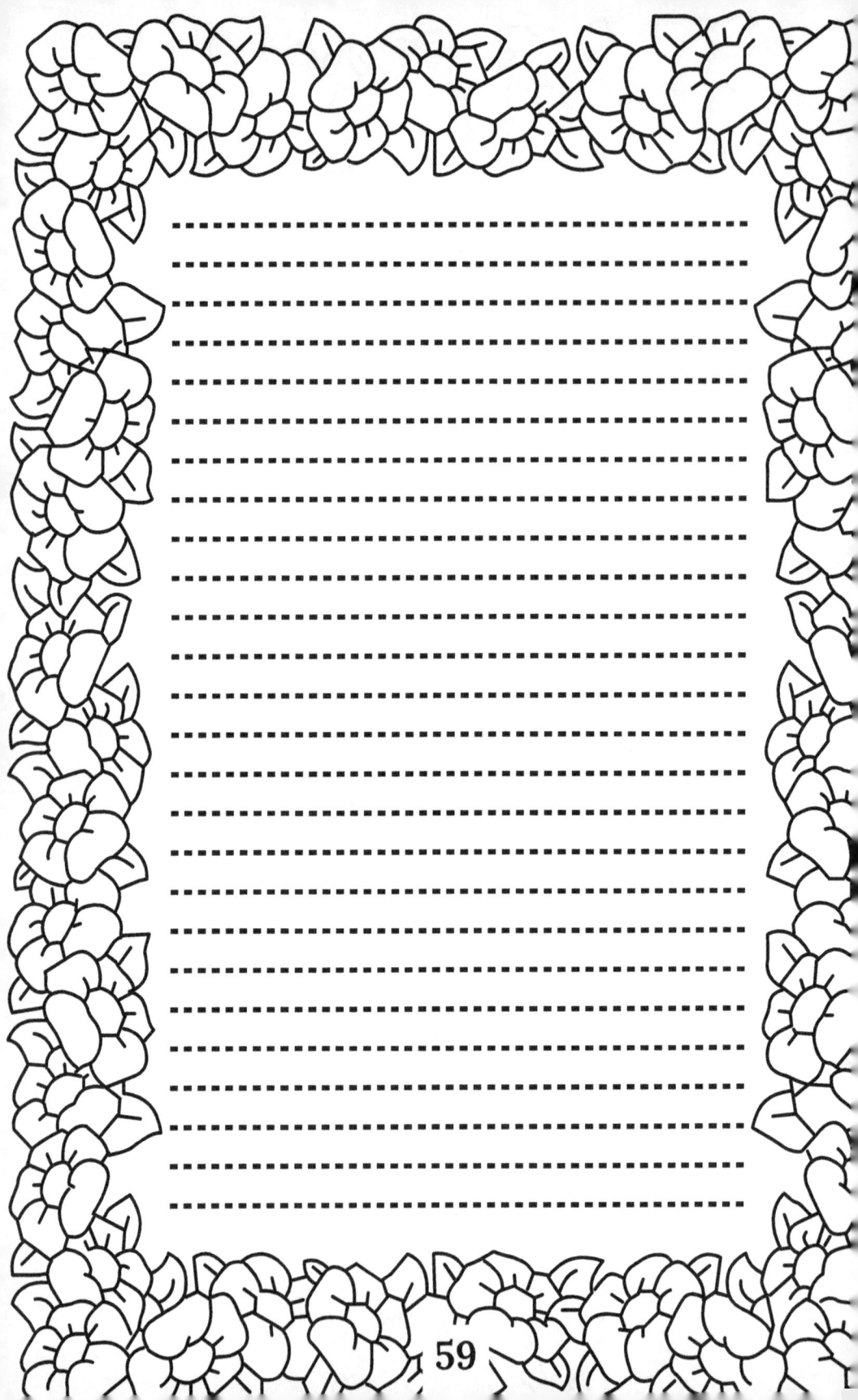

Day: 29

Describe a time when you forgave your sibling.
How did it change you?

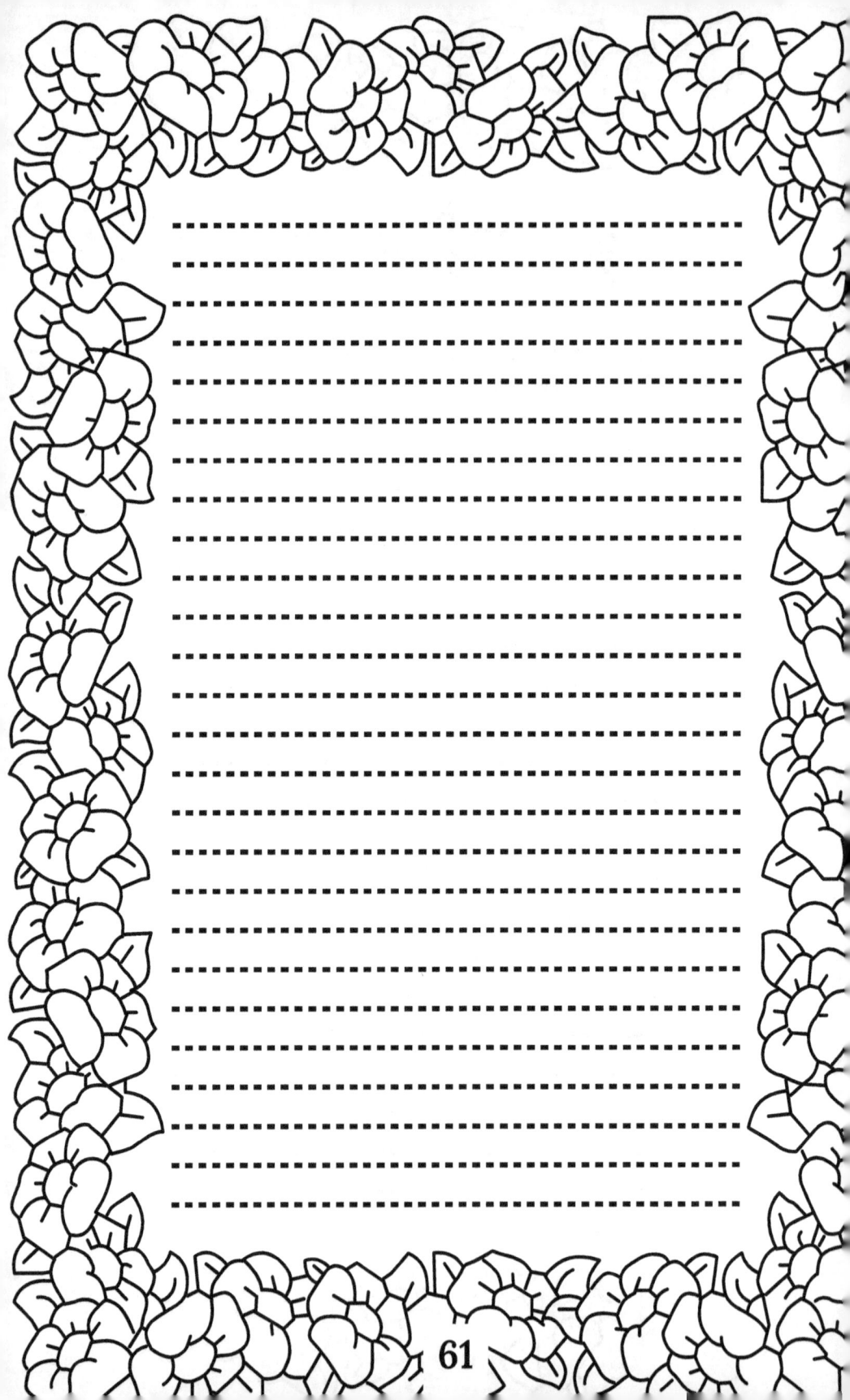

Building Connections

Day: 30

What activities do you enjoy with your siblings?

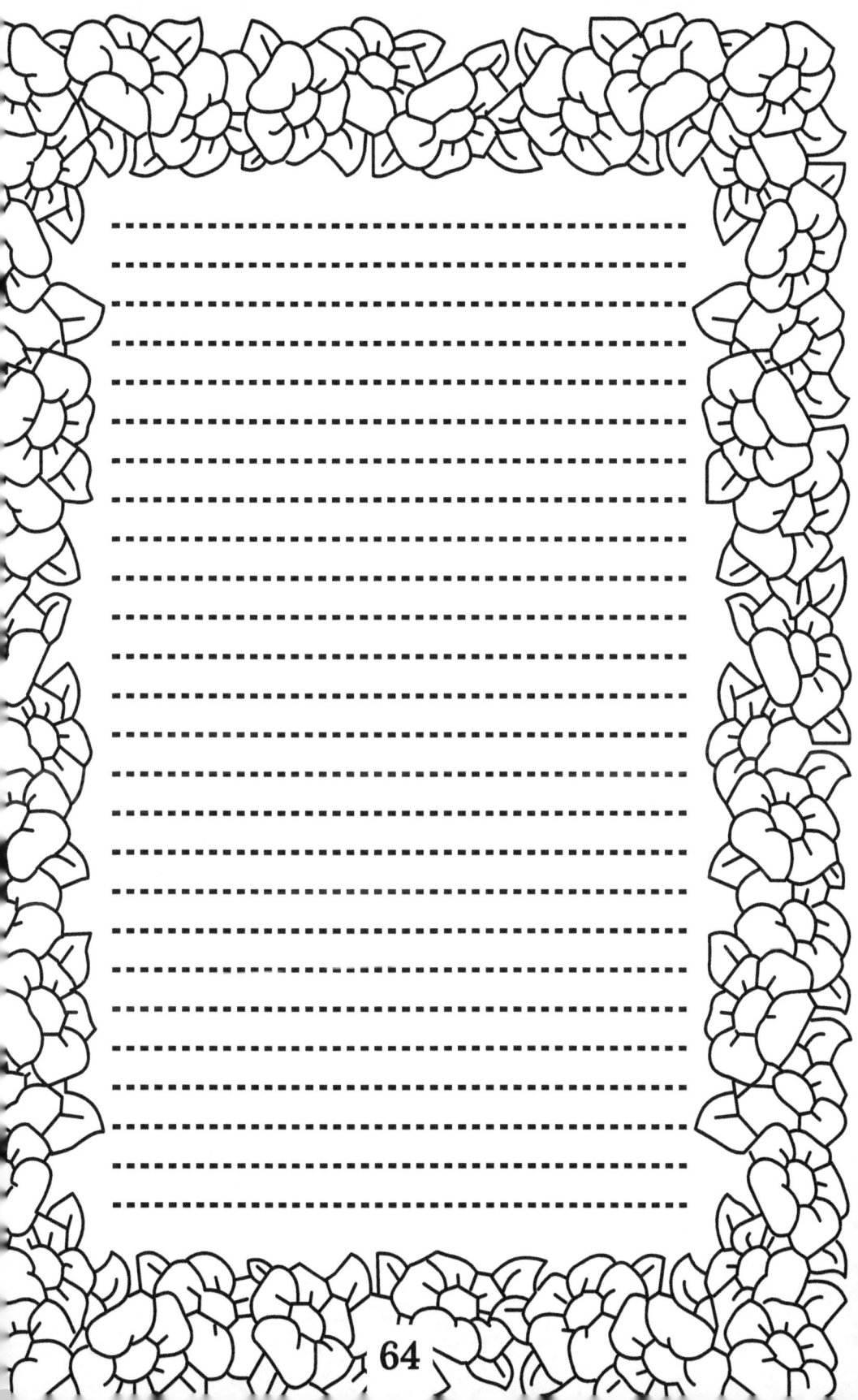

Day: 31

How can you stregthen those bonds moving forward?

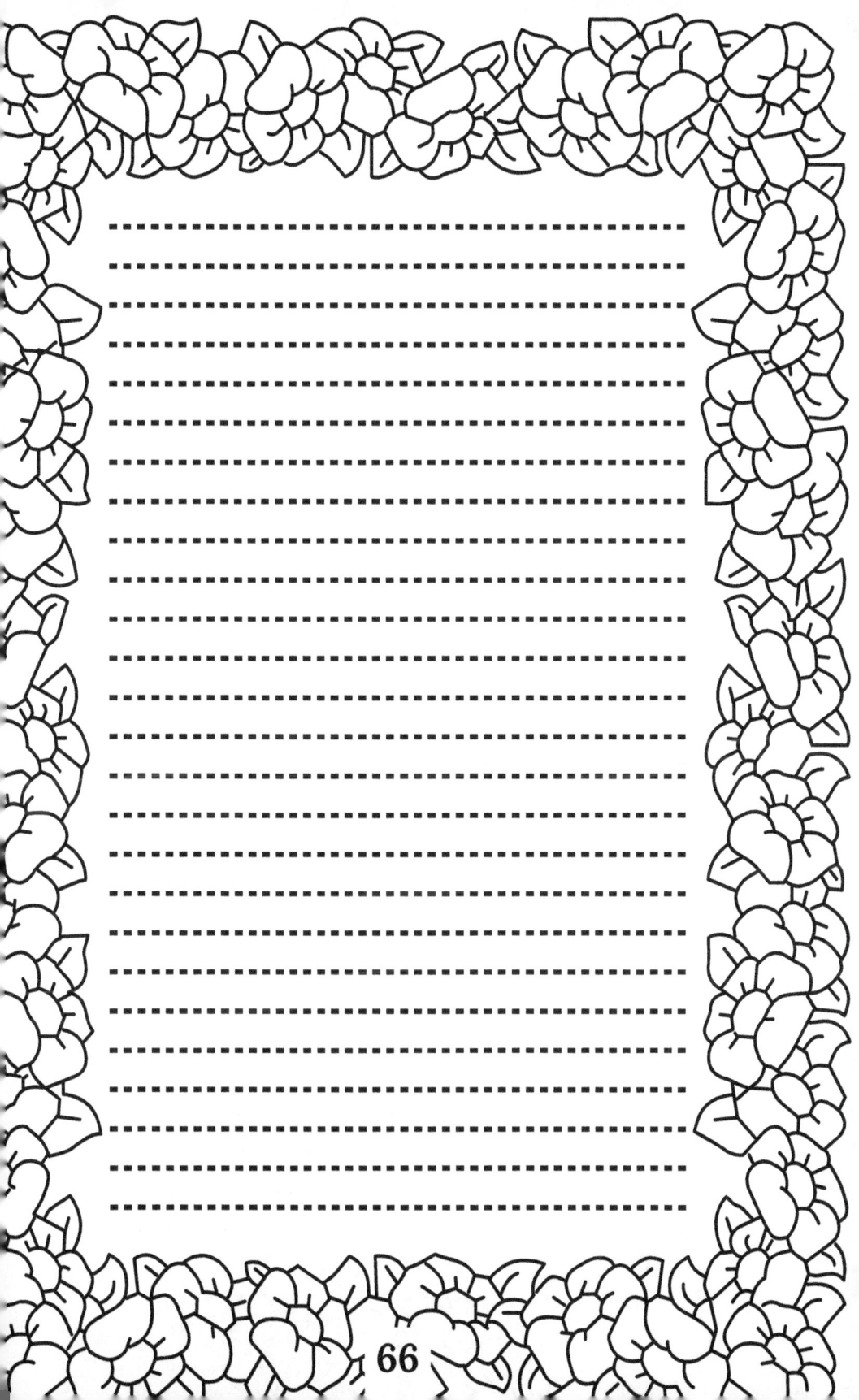

Day: 32

What positive qualities do your siblings possess that you admire?

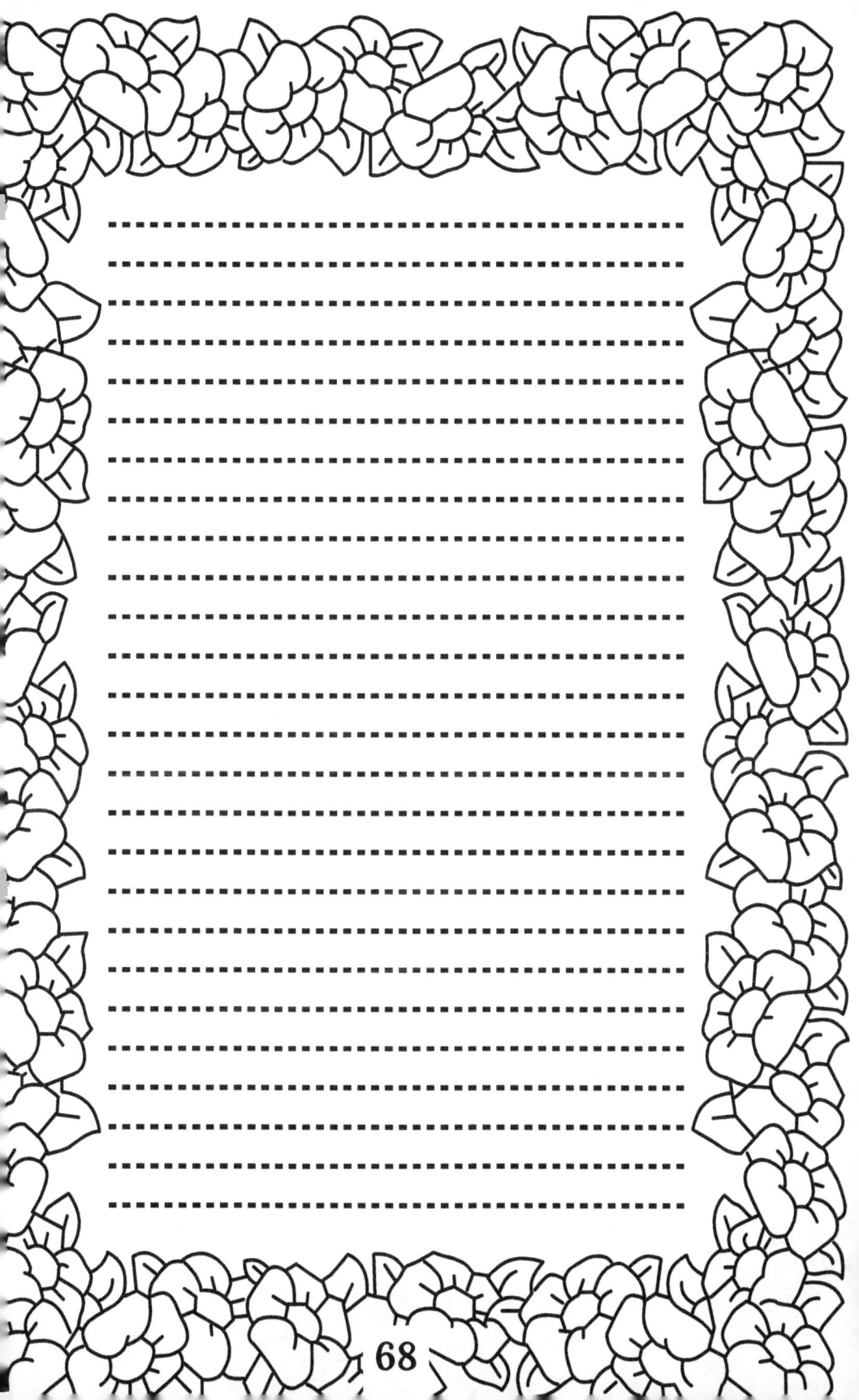

Day: 33

How can you open communication and improve your relationship with your sibling?

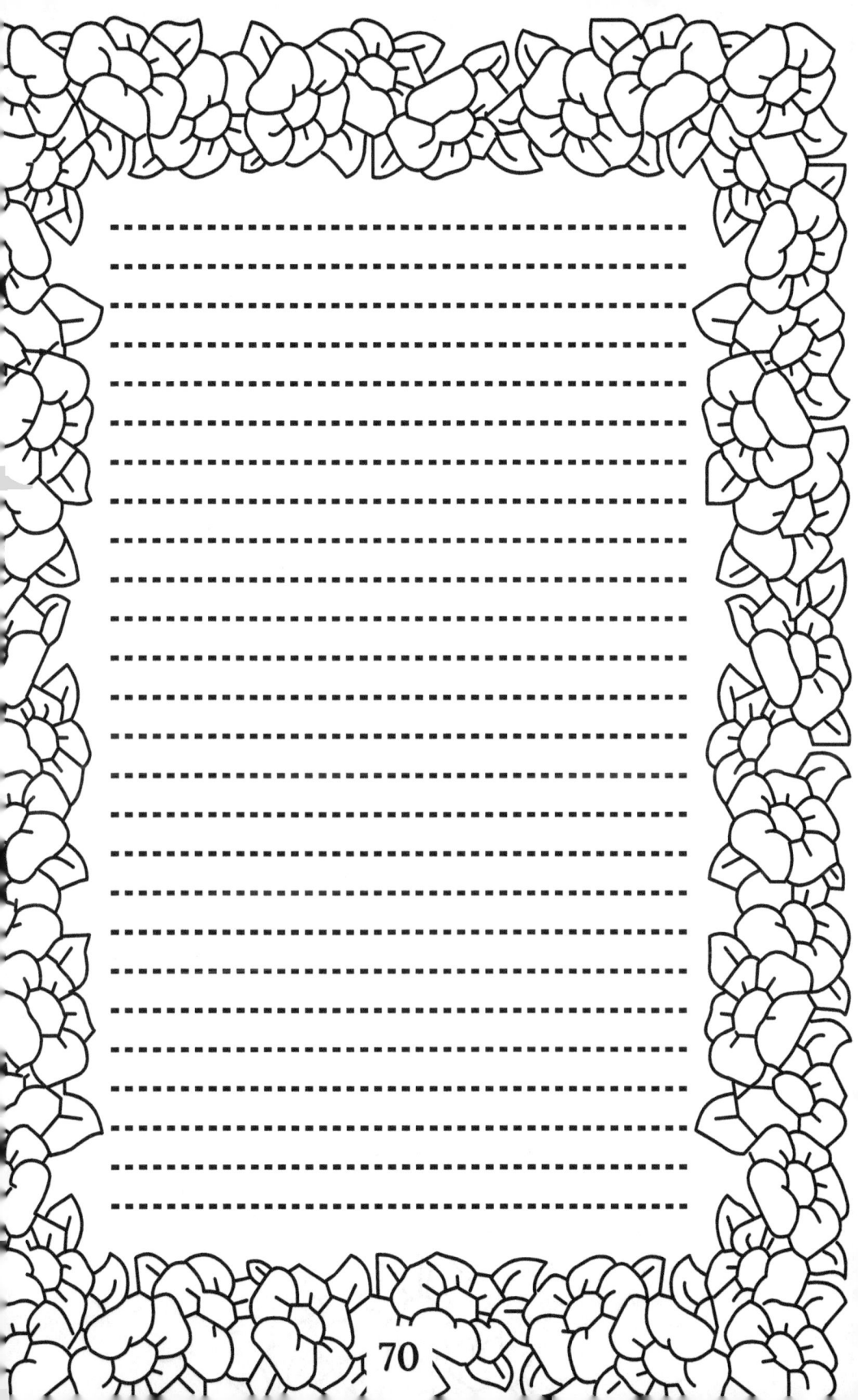

Day: 34

Reflect on a family gathering. What memories stand out?

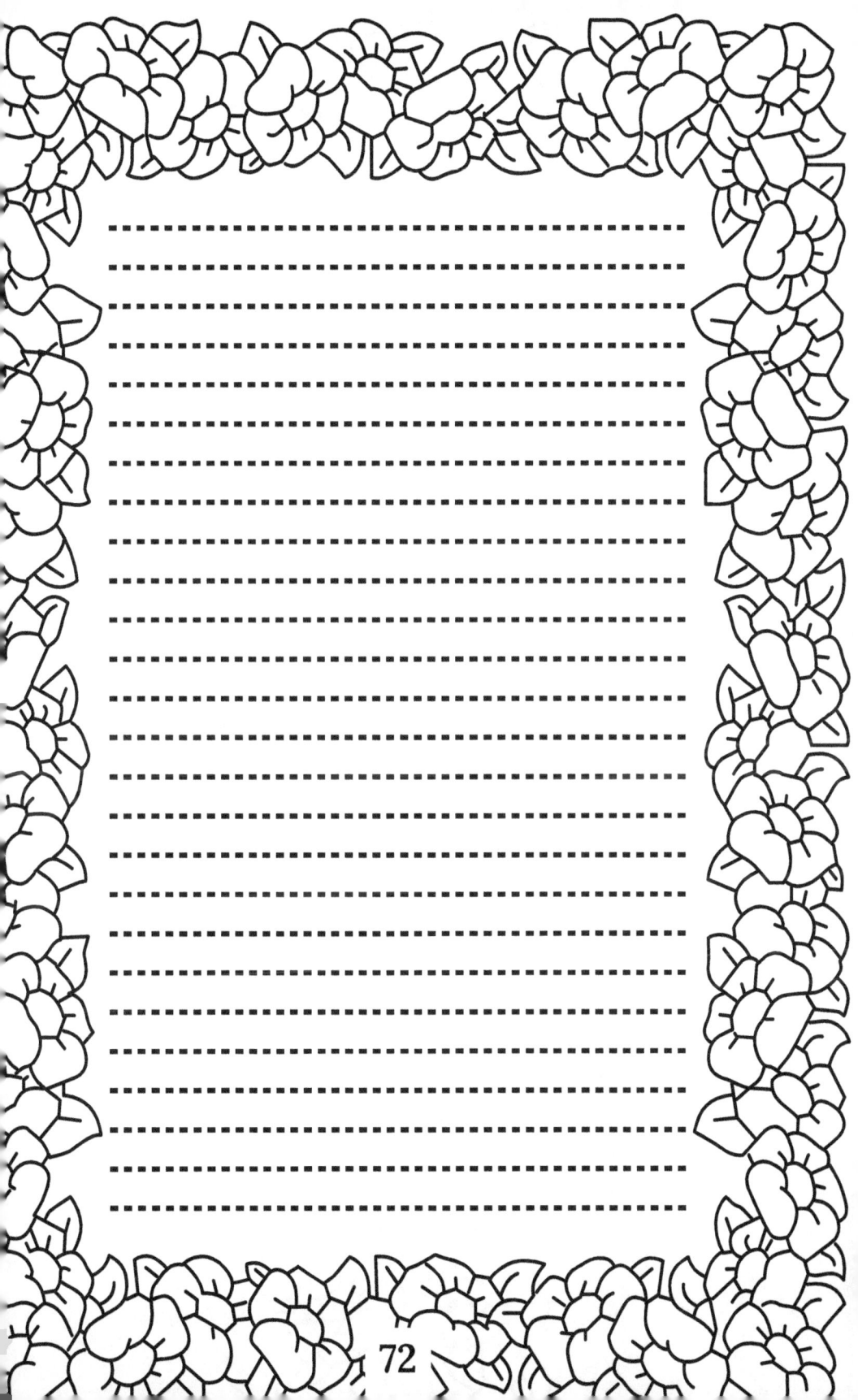

Day: 35

Describe a time when you learned something valuable from a sibling.

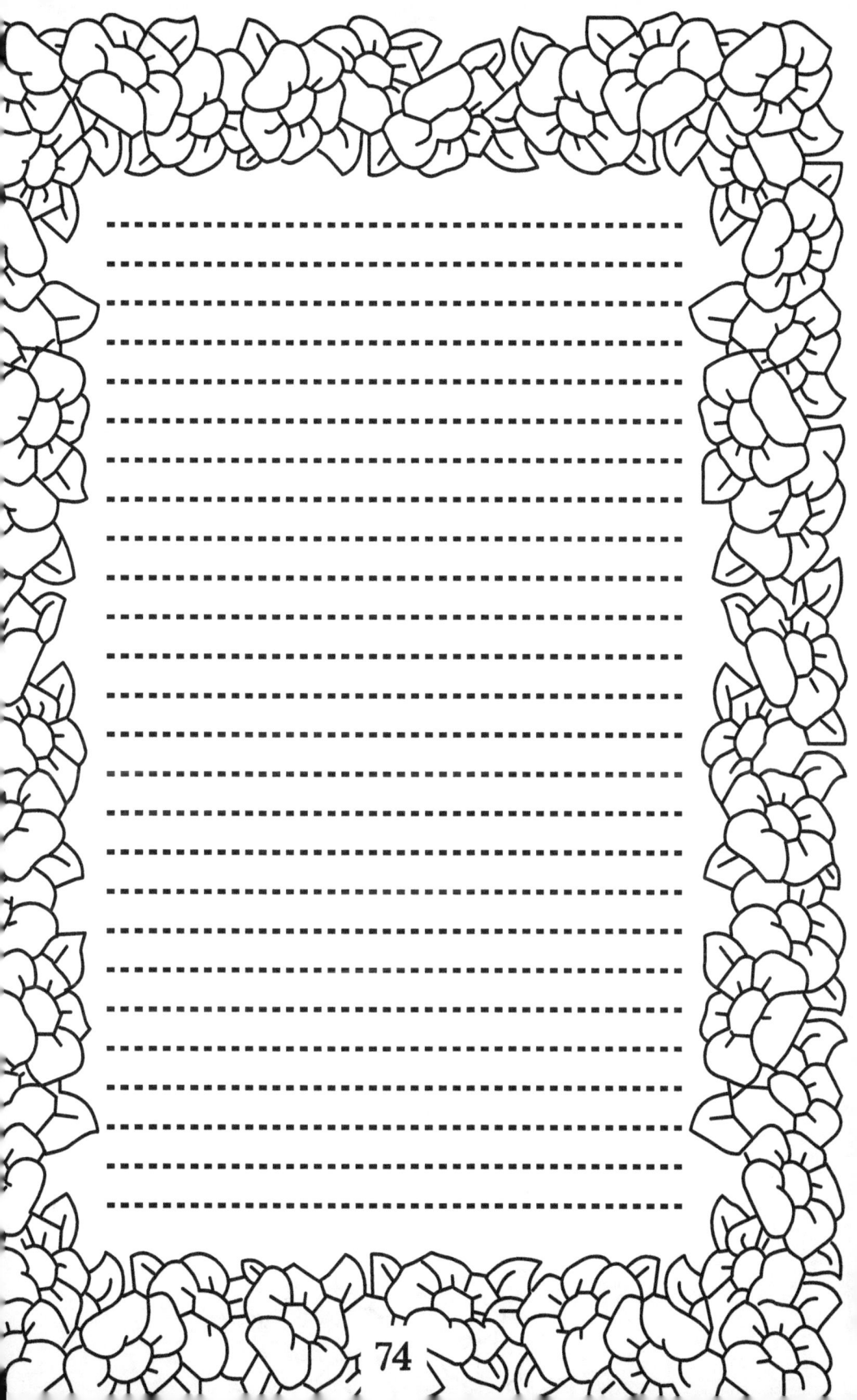

Day: 36

What role do you want your siblings to play in your life in the future?

....
....
....
....
....
....
....
....
....
....
....
....
....
....
....
....
....
....
....
....
....
....

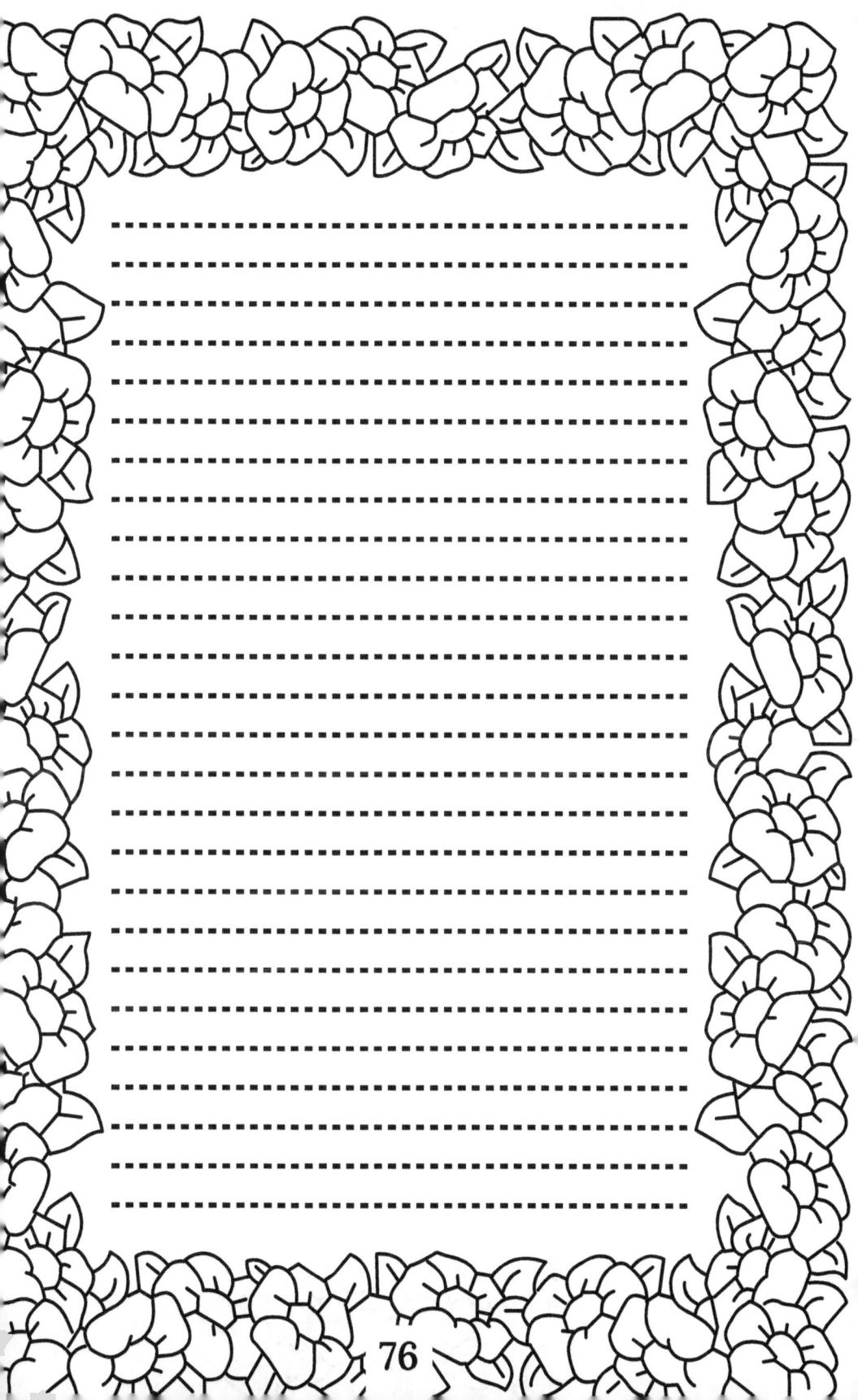

Moving Forward

Day: 37

Reflect on how you can be a better sibling.

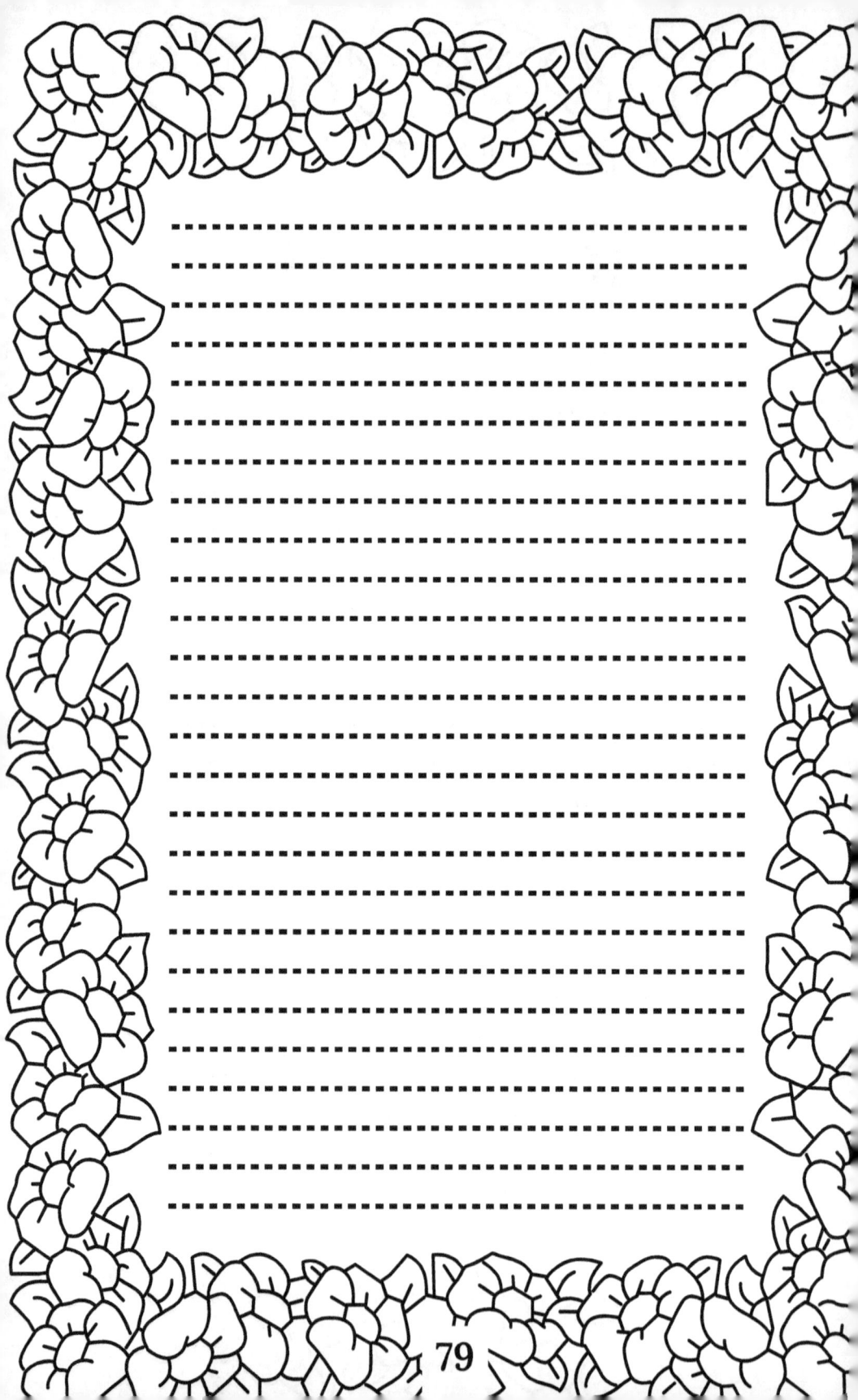

Day: 38

What are some changes you can make to assist with this process?

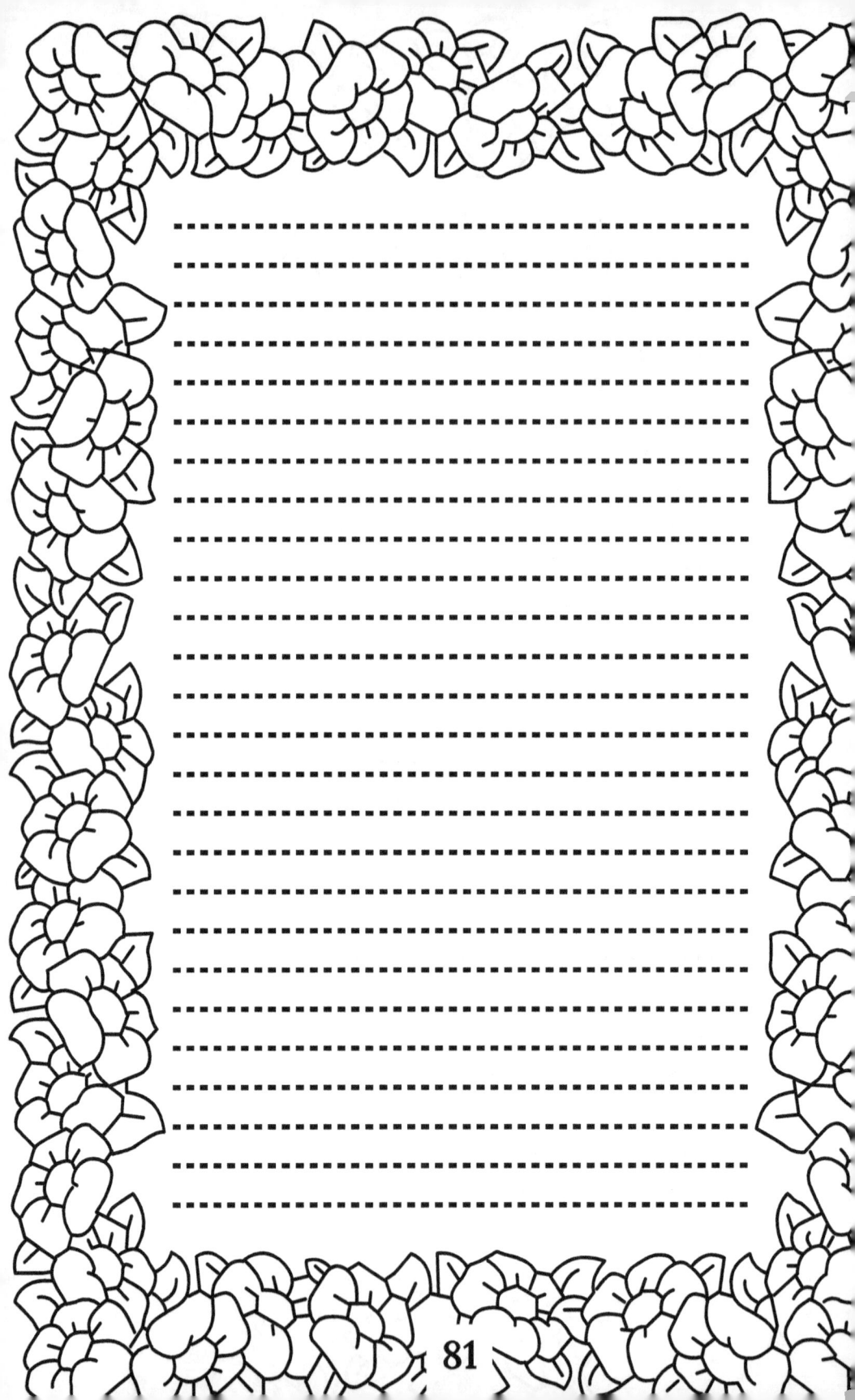

Day: 39

What are some boundaries that you need to set with your siblings, if any?

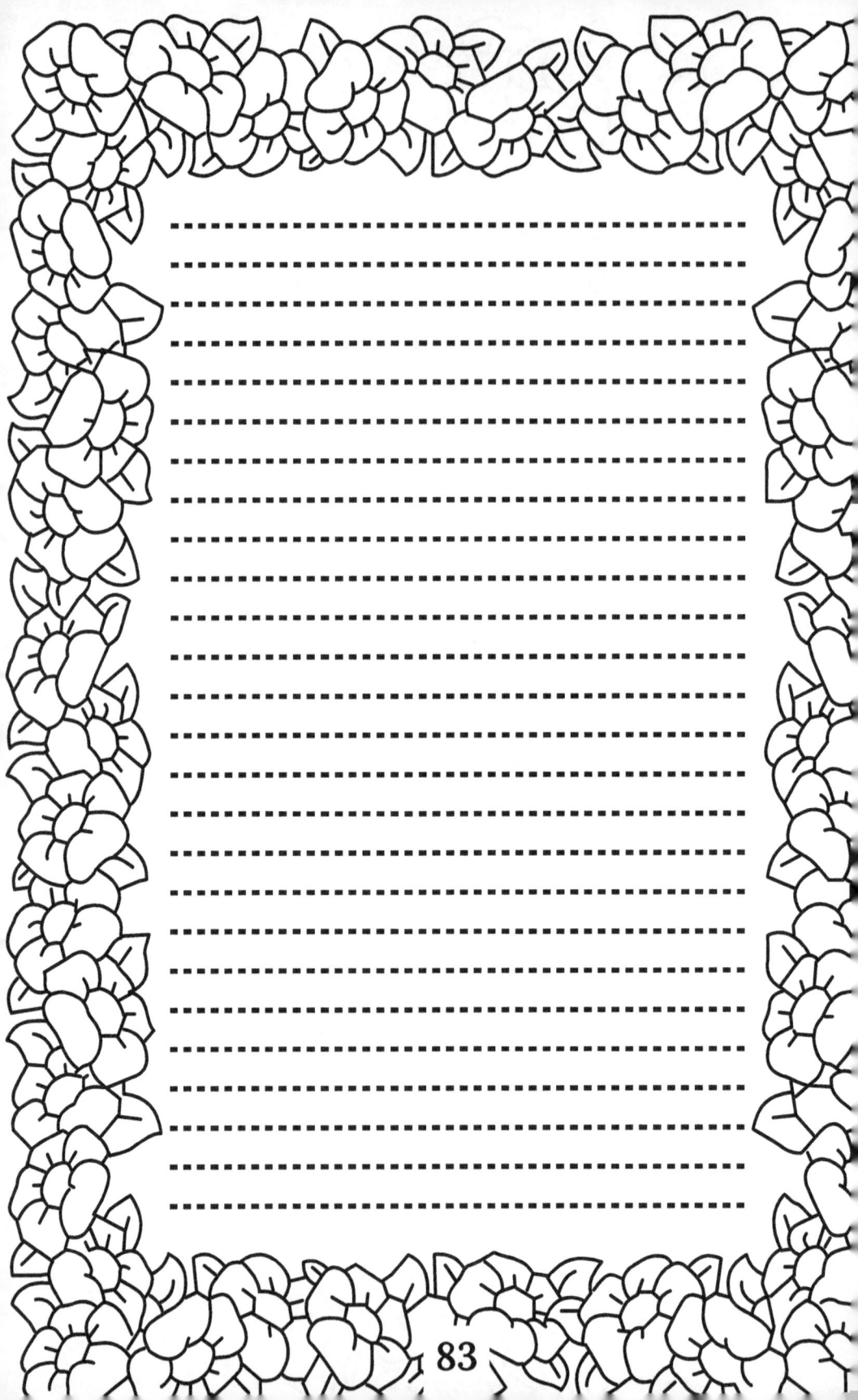

Day: 40

What are your hopes for your sibling relationship in the next year?

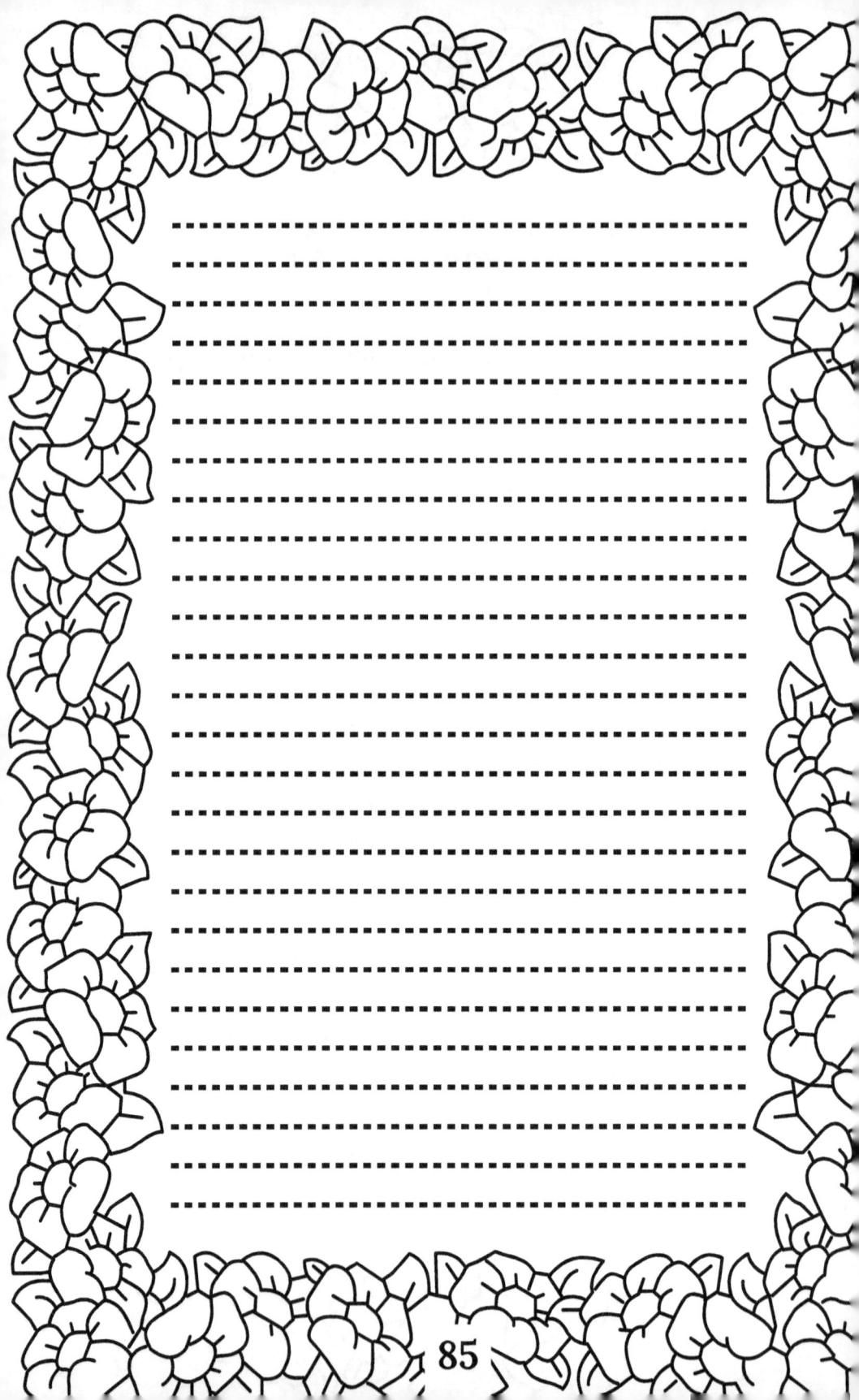

Day: 41

What past conflicts inform your future interactions?

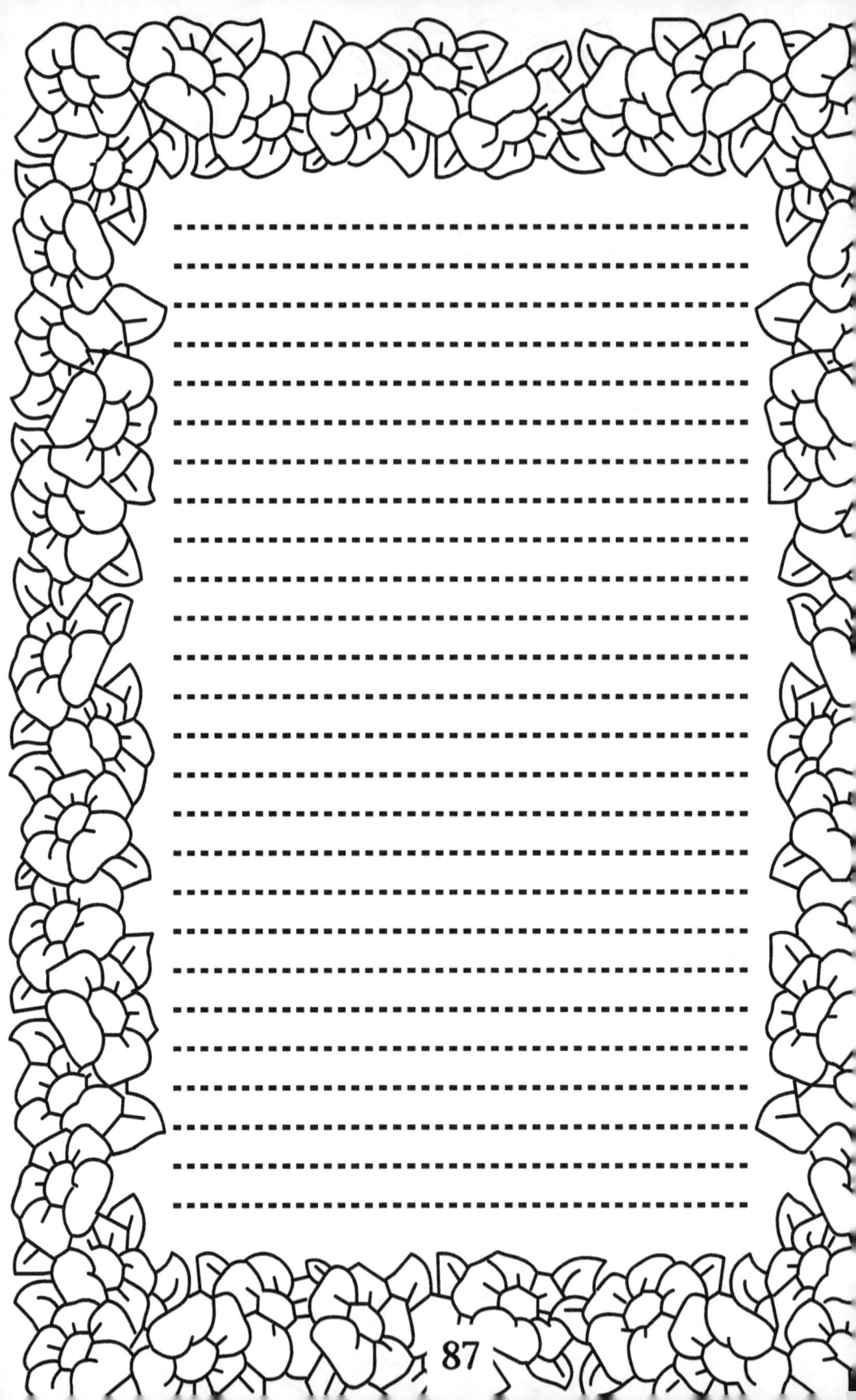

Day: 42

What are some ways that you can express gratitude towards your siblings?

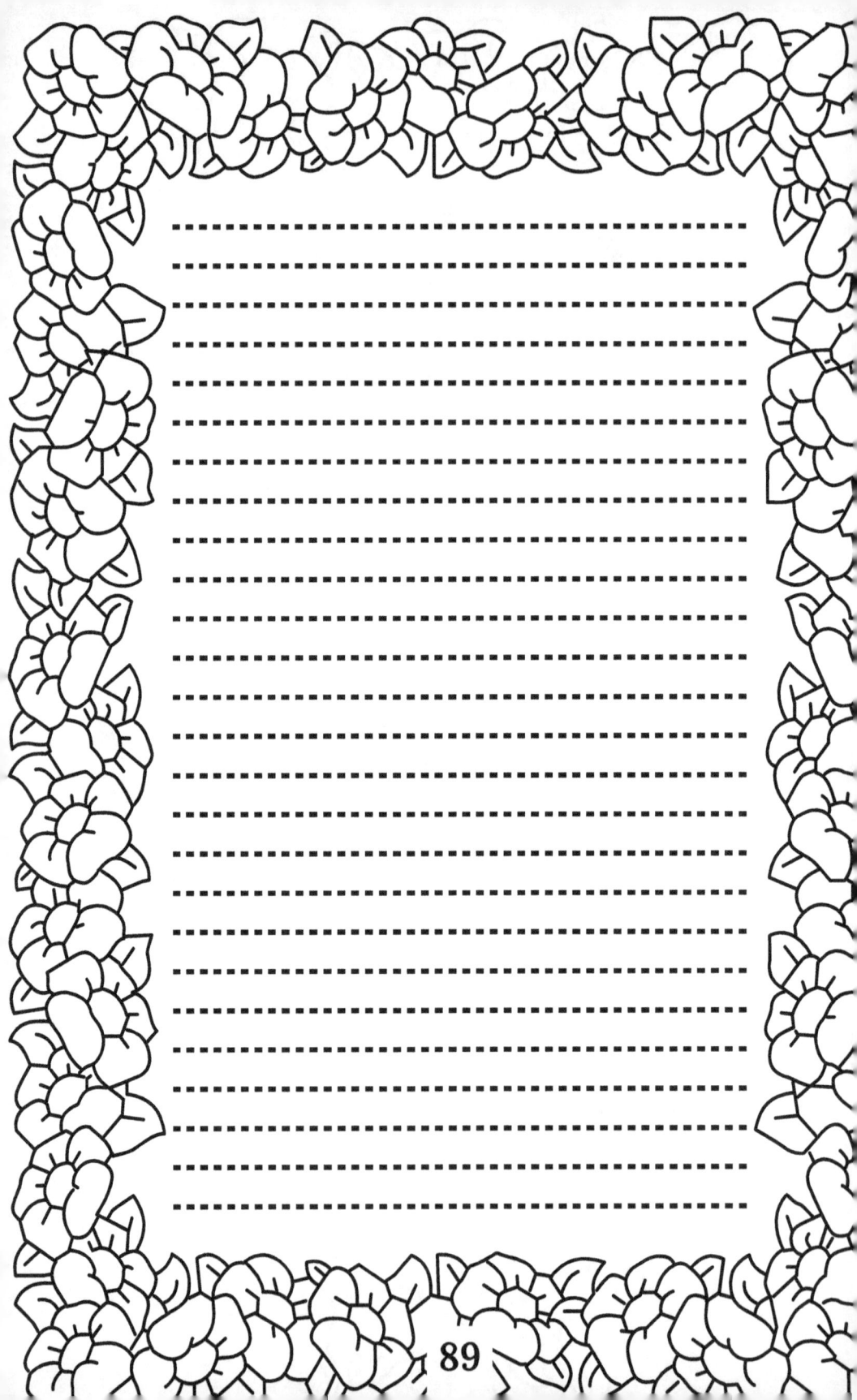

Day: 43

What positive affirmations can you create for yourself in regards to your family?

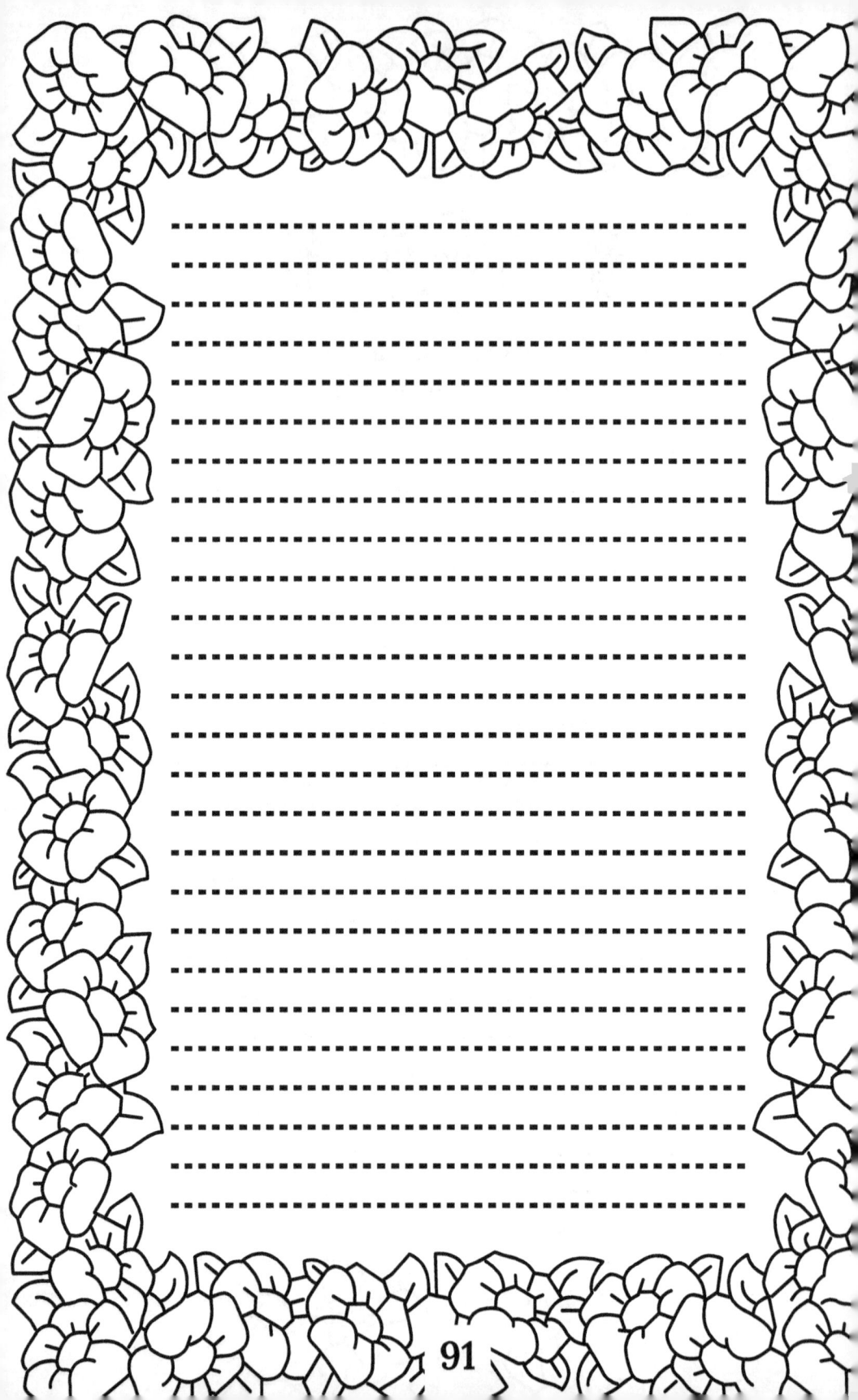

Day: 44

Write about a time that you felt extremly proud of your siblings.

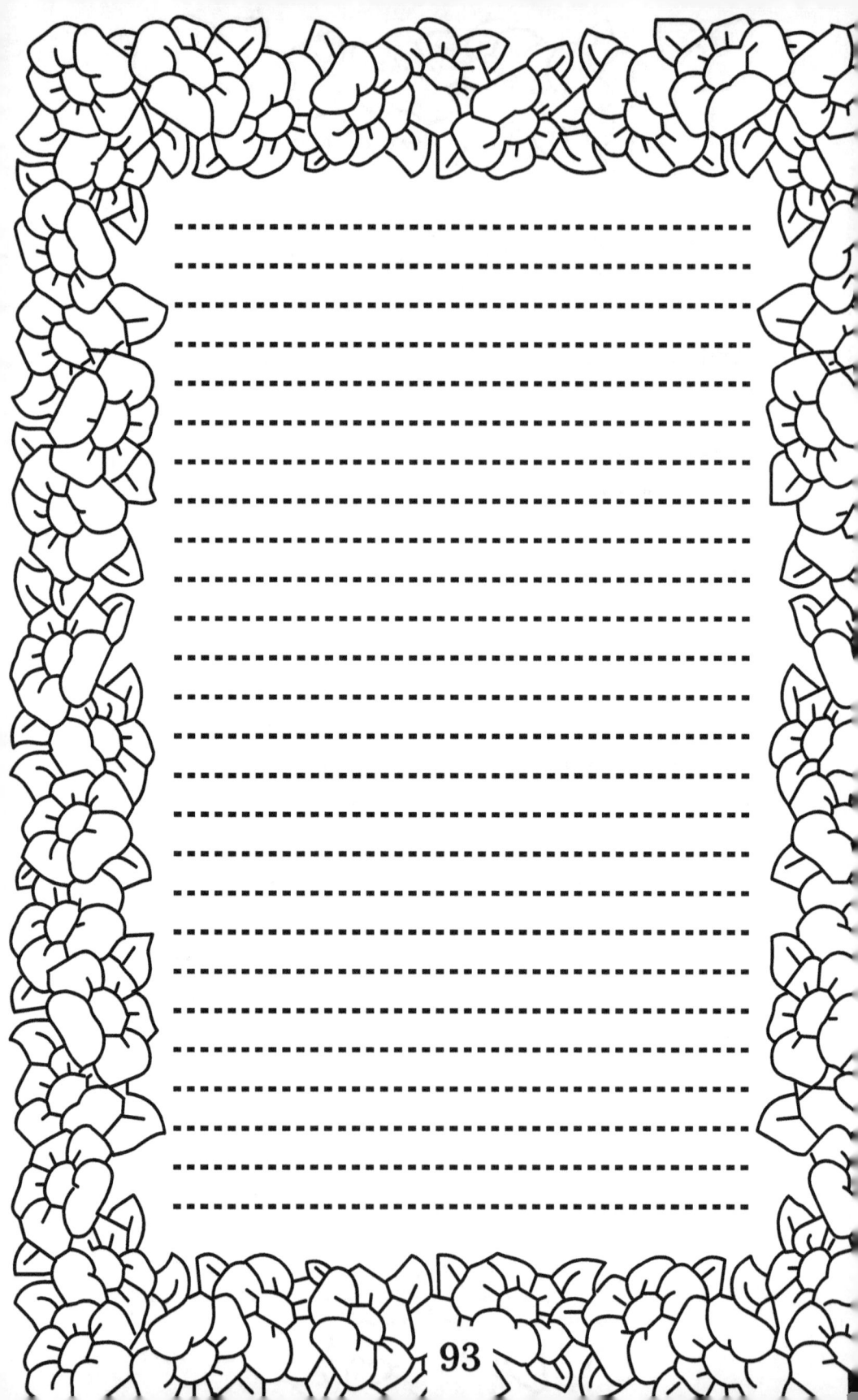

Day: 45

Why did you choose this memory?

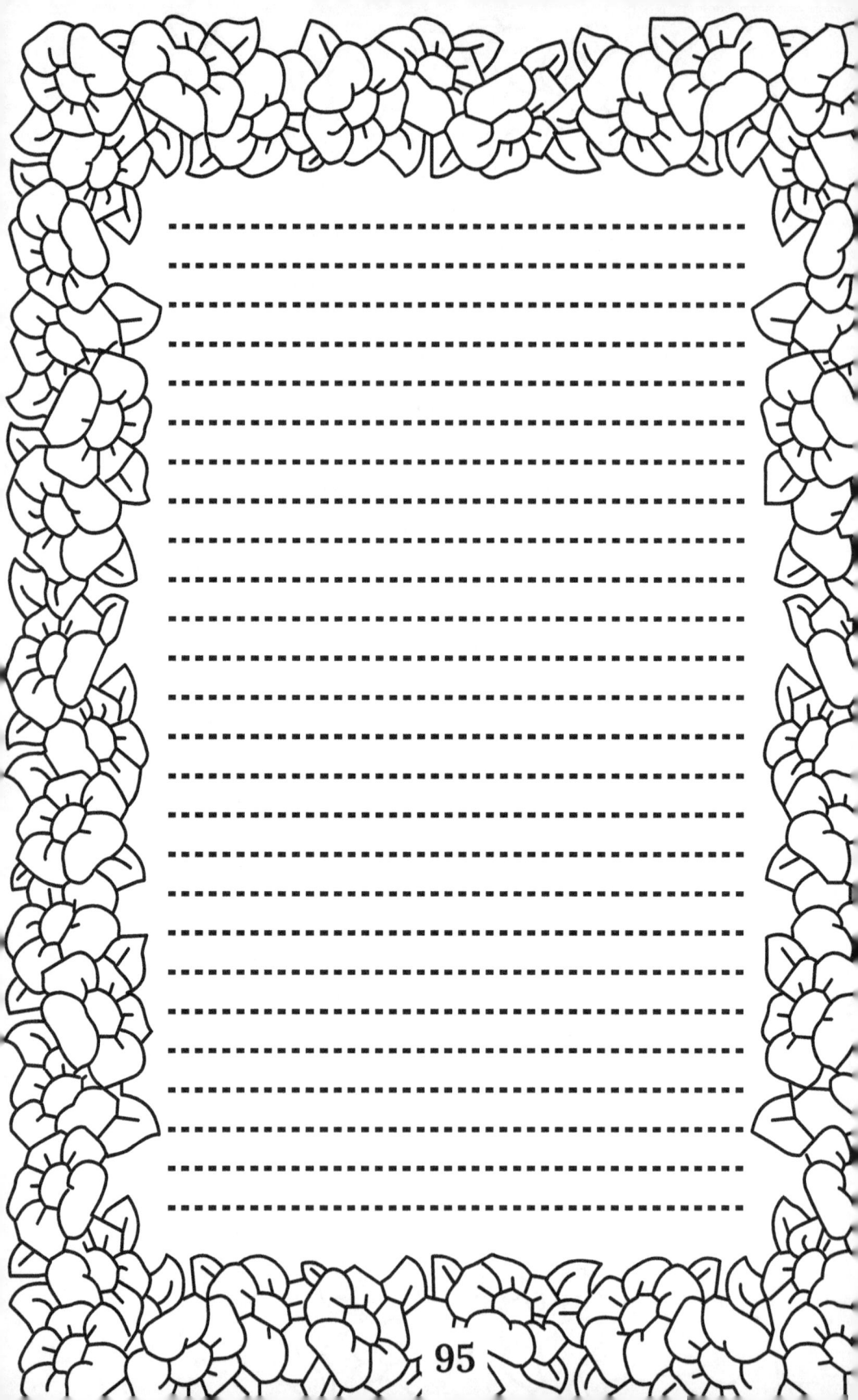

Self
Discovery

Day: 46

What is your family's communication style?

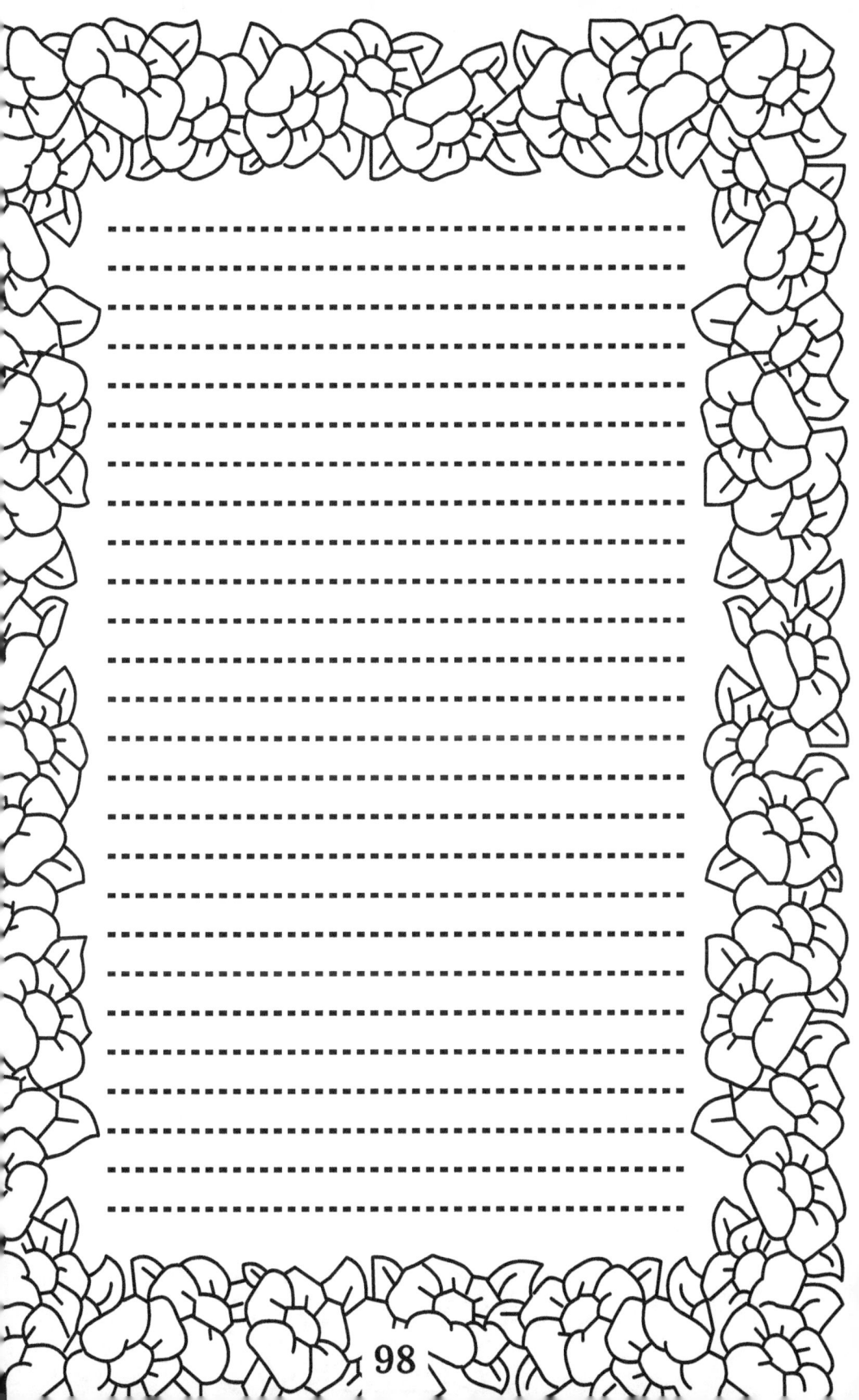

Day: 47

Describe how it affects you.

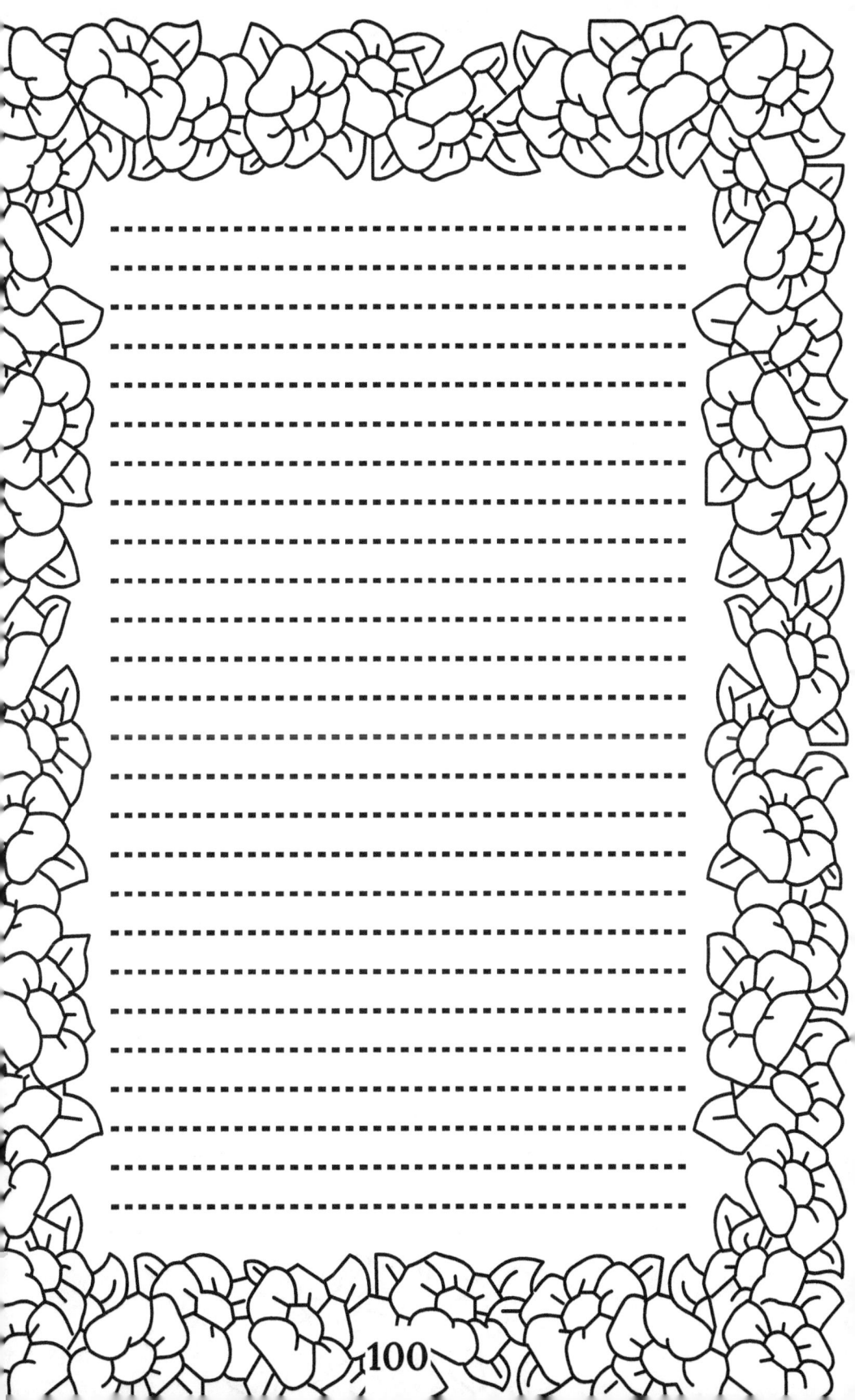

Day: 48

Has your relationship with your sibling shaped your identity? Describe how .

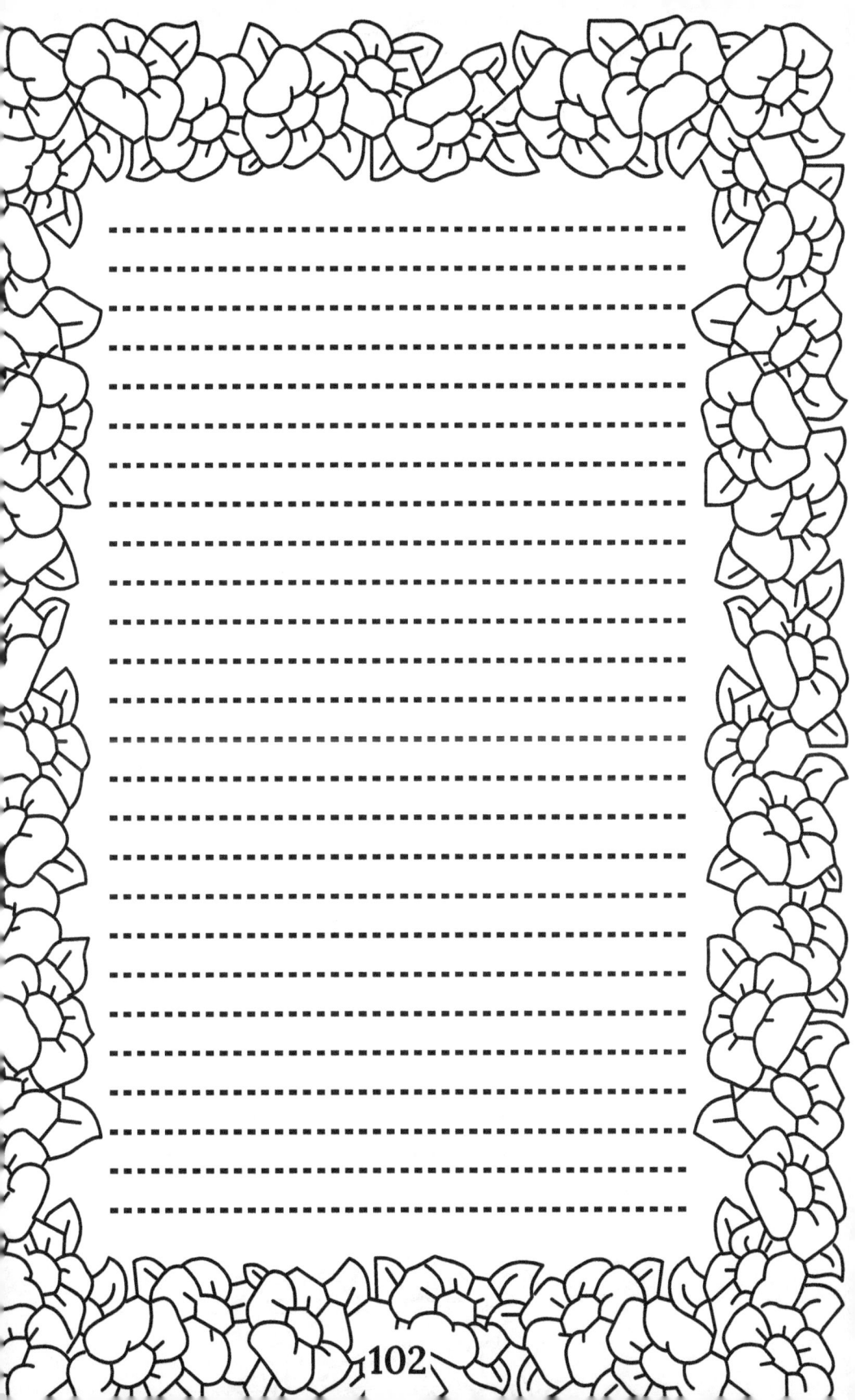

Day: 49

Describe how your ideal relationship with your sibling would look if you had limited conflict.

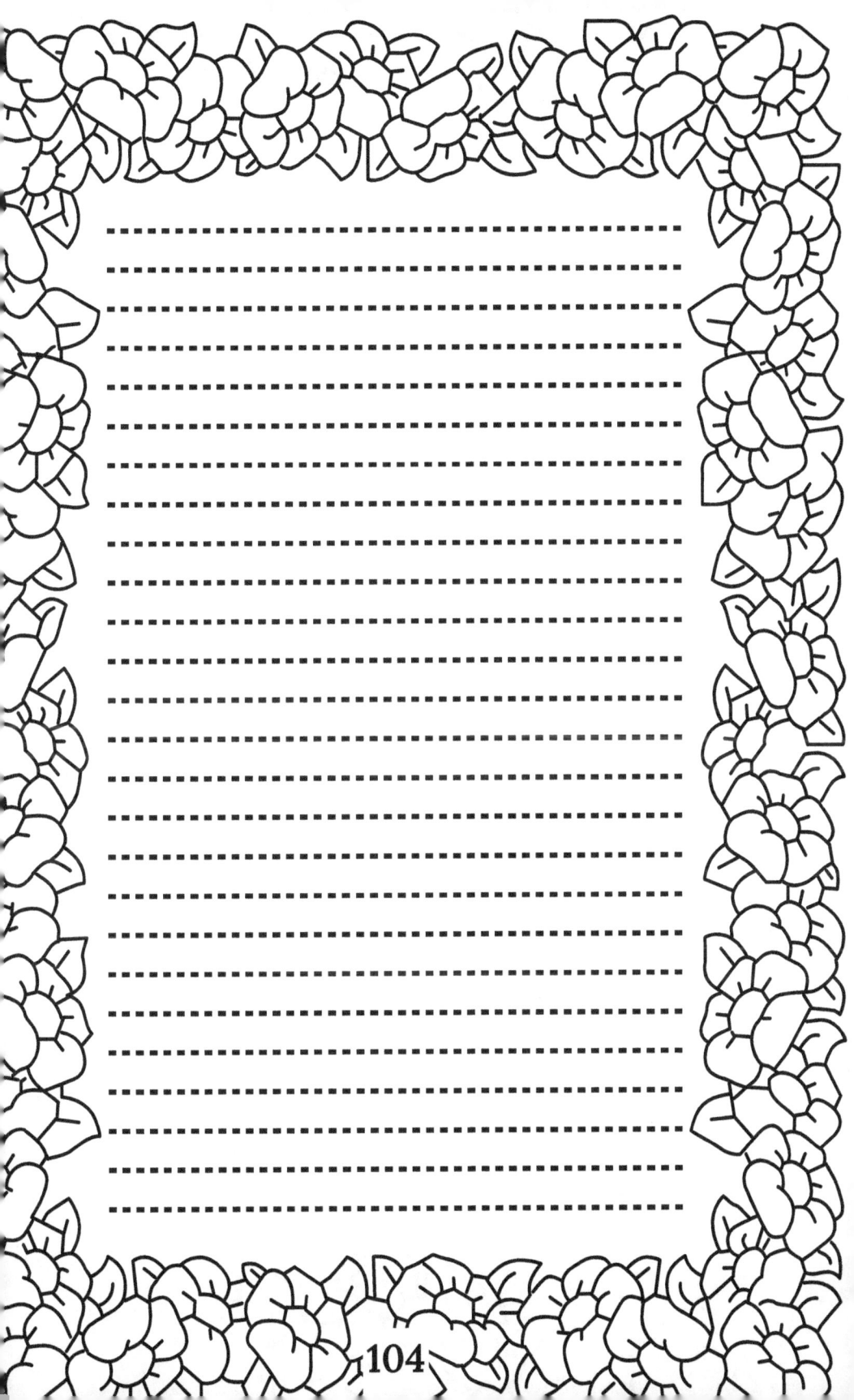

What roles does vulnerability play in your relationship with your siblings.?

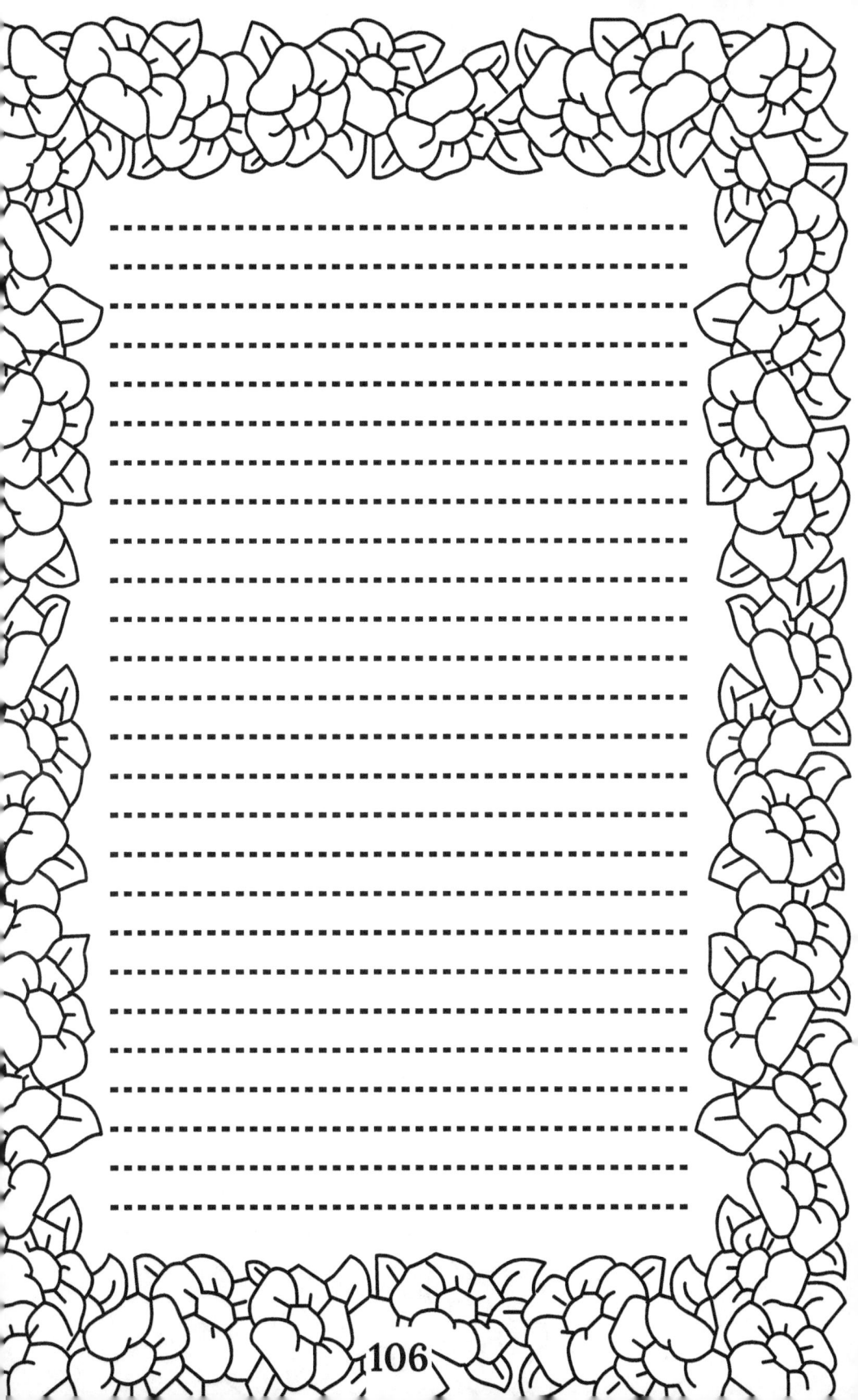

Day: 51

Does jealousy or competition play a major role in your sibling relationship? Describe how it causes conflict.

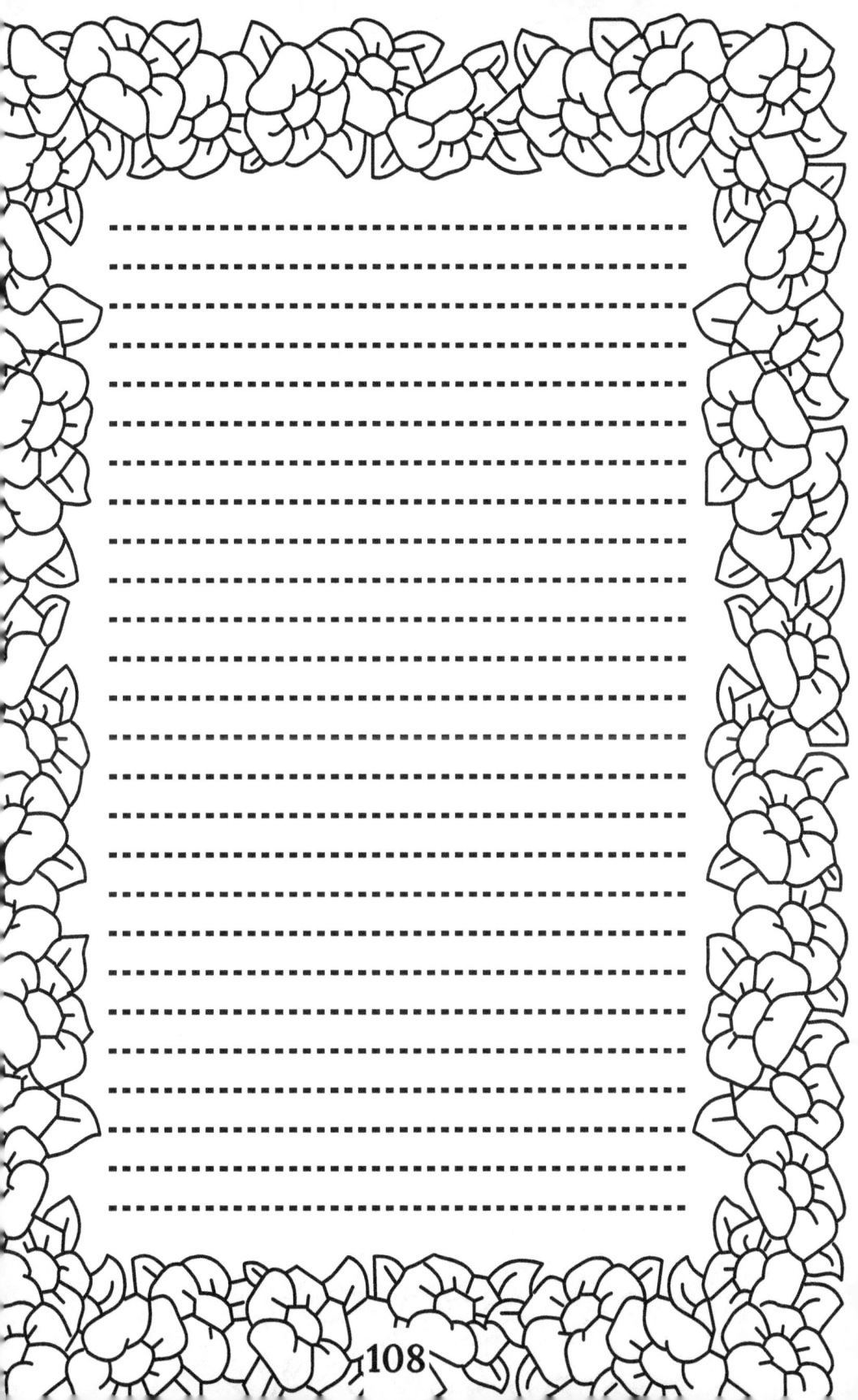

Day: 52

What would you like to say to your inner child about your sibling relationship?

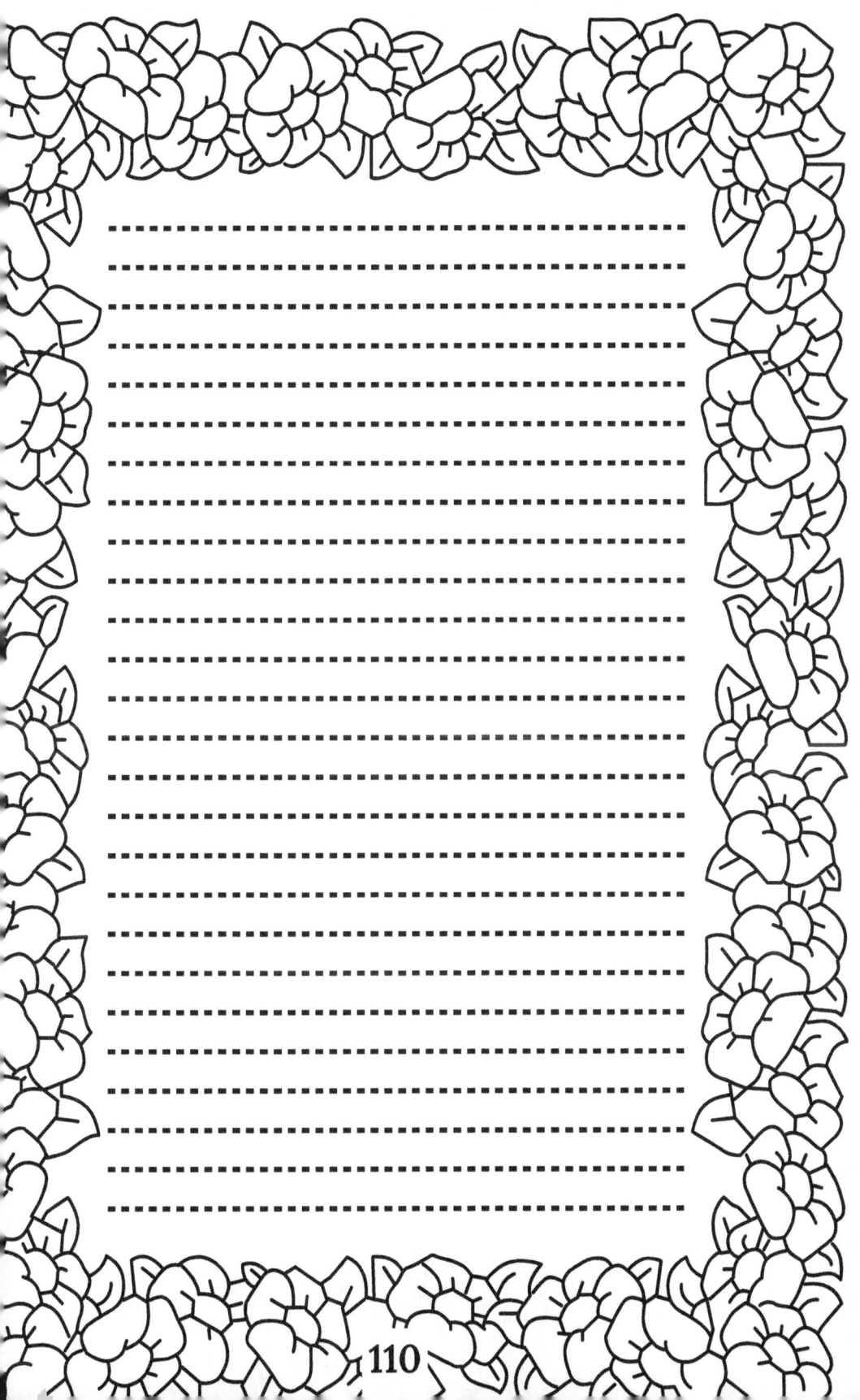

Reflection
and Growth

Day: 53

Write about five things that you have learned about yourself throughout this journaling process.

Day: 54

Describe any changes that you have experiencd
or noticed in your feelings about your siblings
over the past weeks..

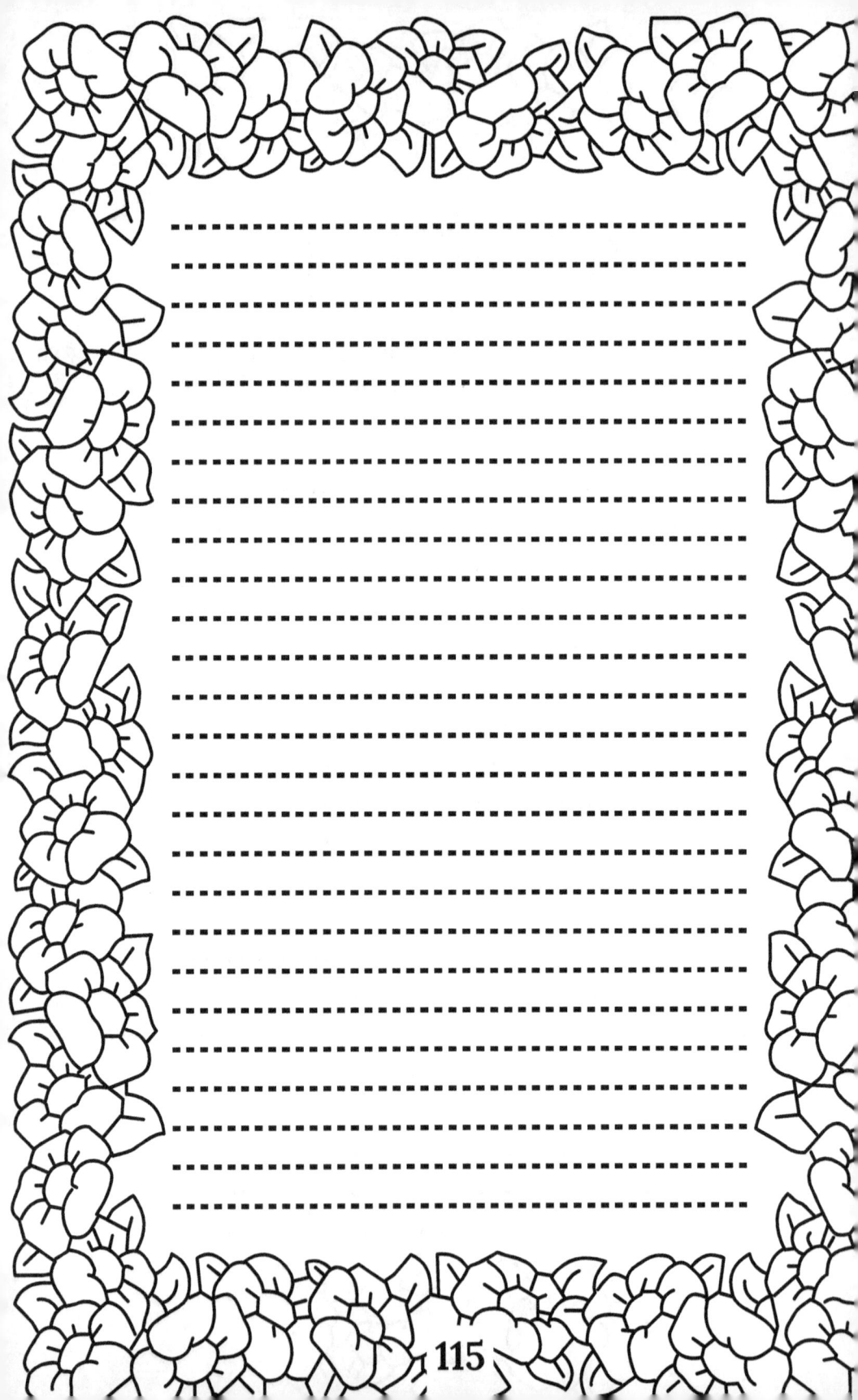

Day: 55

Describe how you plan to keep working on your sibling relationship in the future.

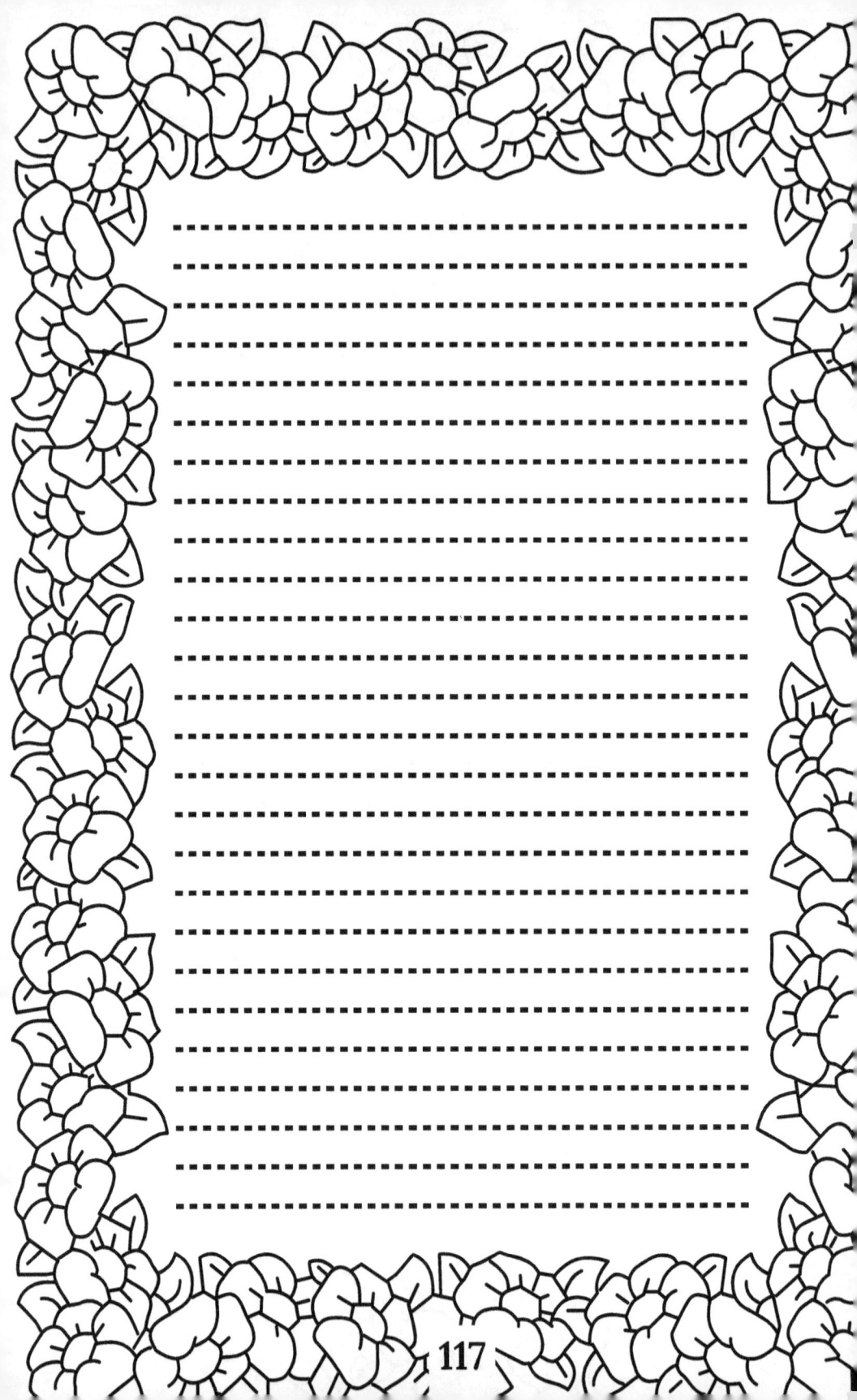

Day: 56

What legacy do you want to create within your family?

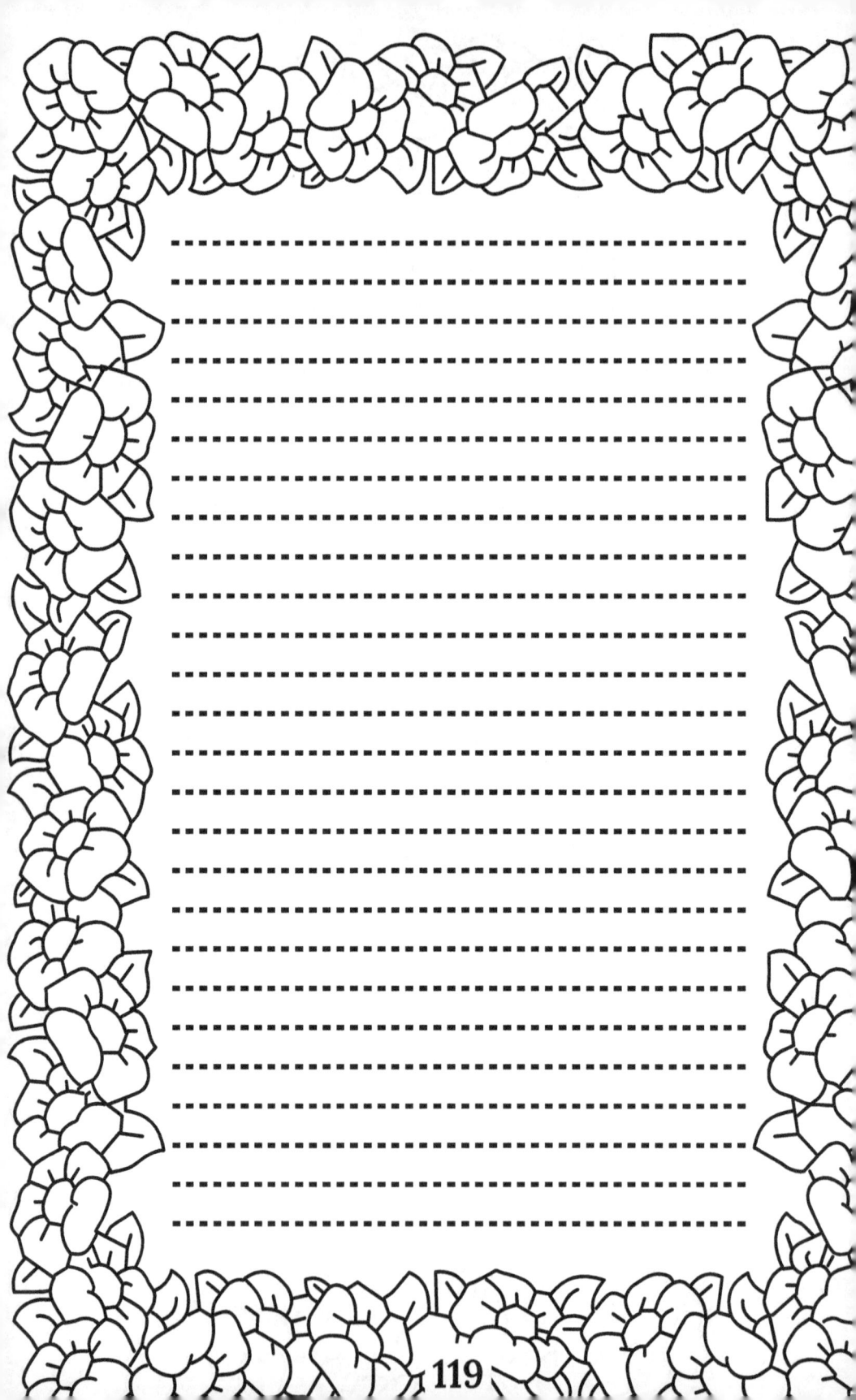

Closing
Thoughts

Day: 57

How has your understanding of Soul Wounds evolved?

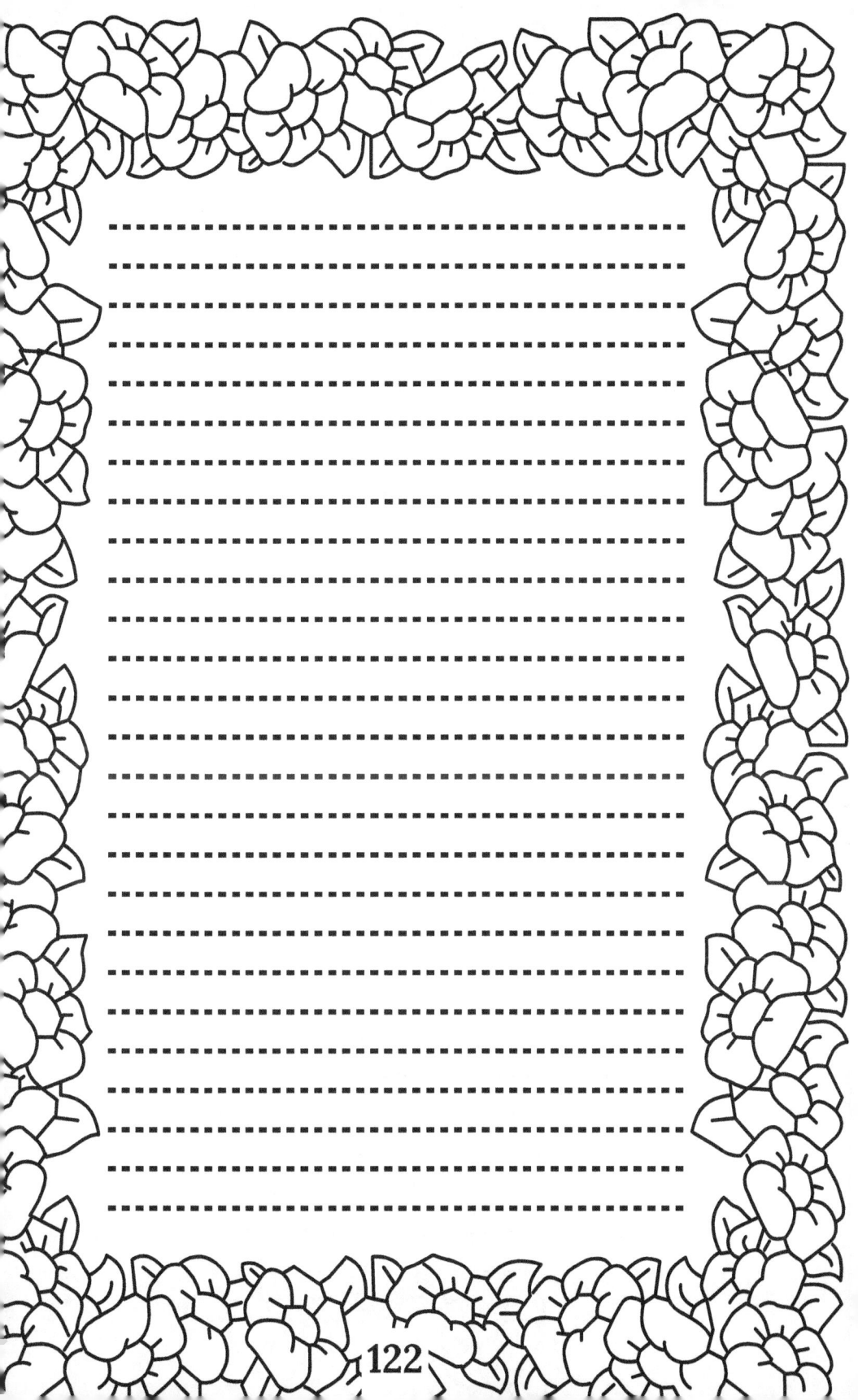

Day: 58

What do you hope to achieve by continuing to work on your sibling relationship?

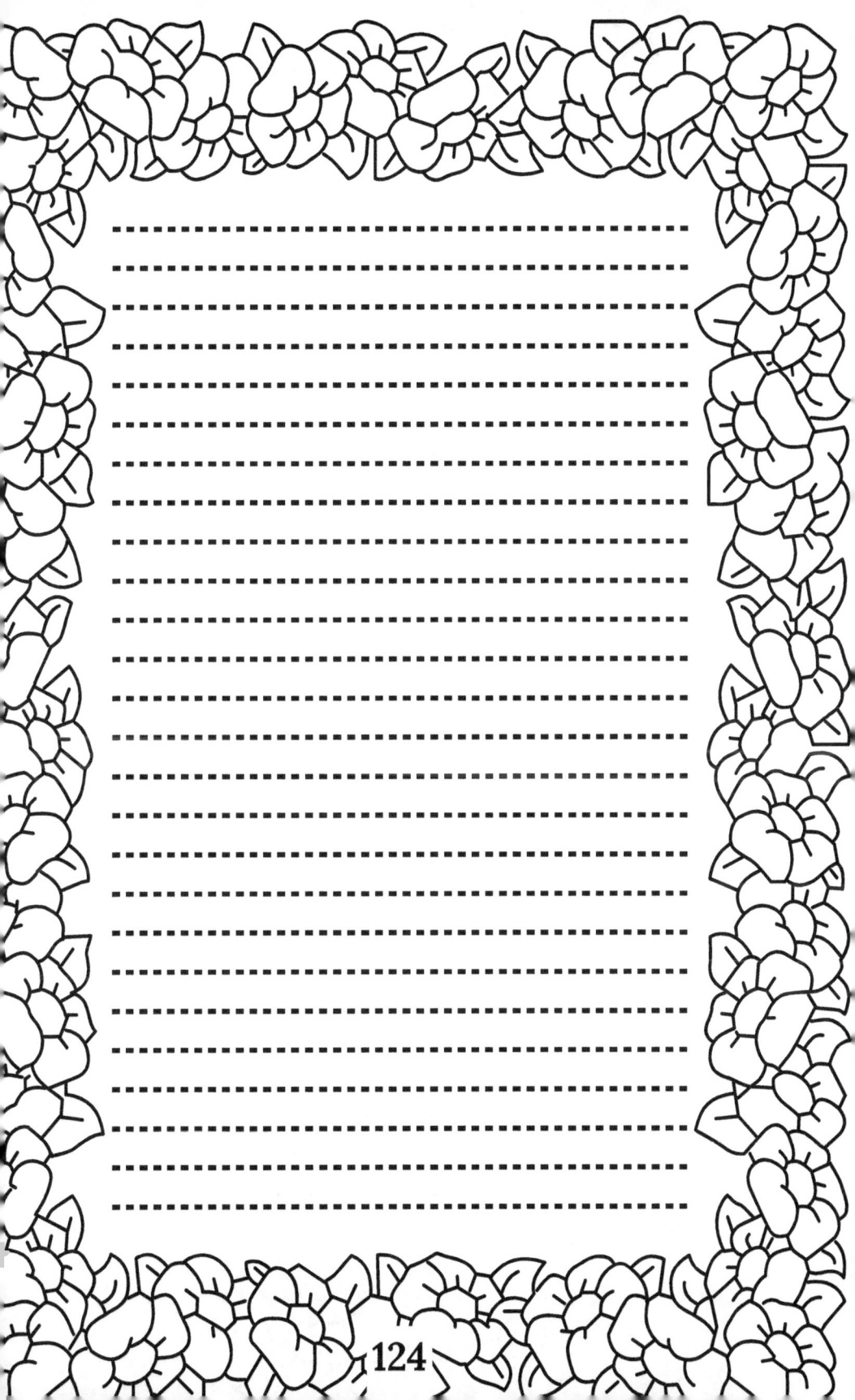

Day: 59

Write a letter to your sibling expressing your thoughts on your journey.

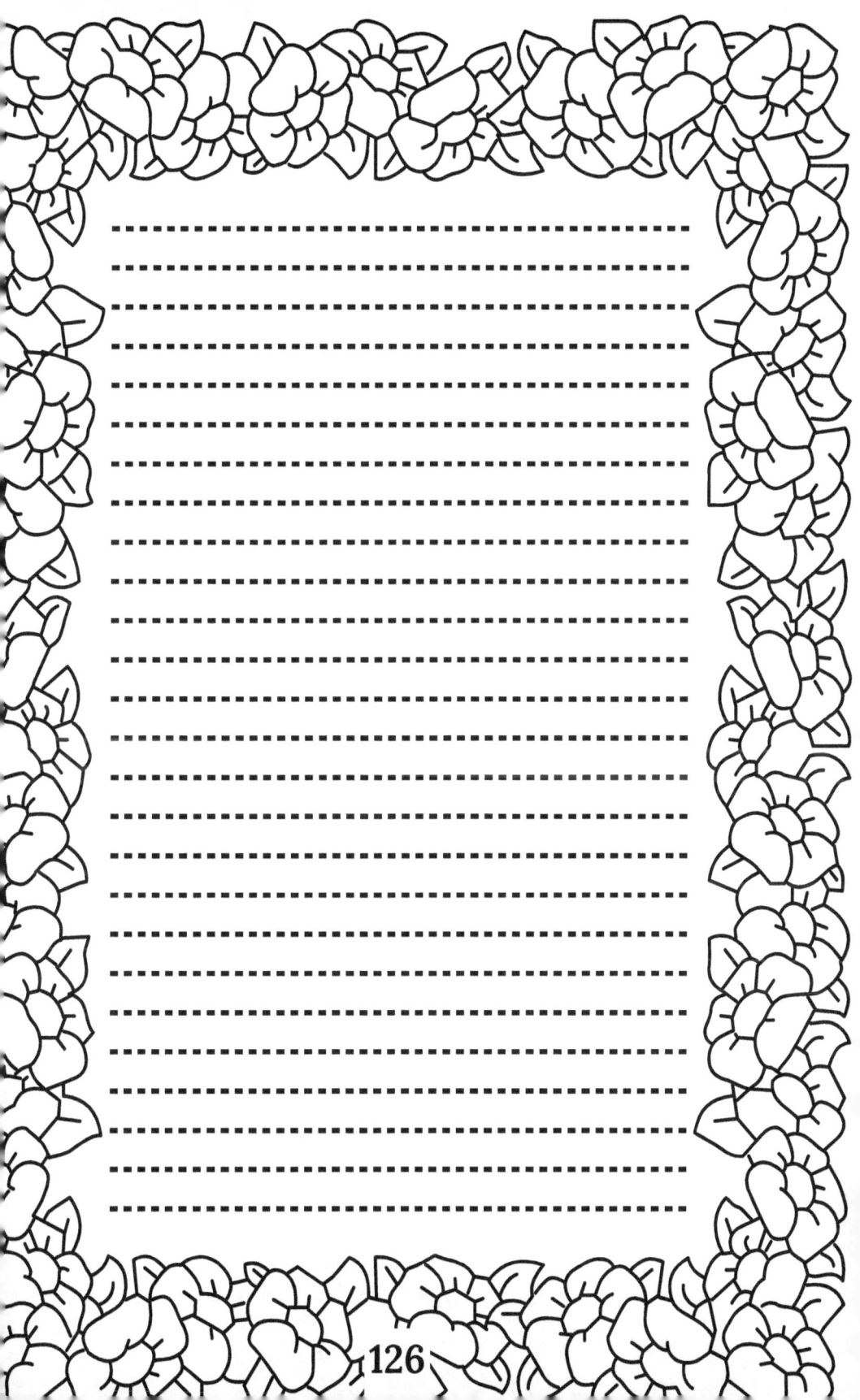

Day: 60

Reflect on this journaling experience. What was most impactful for you?

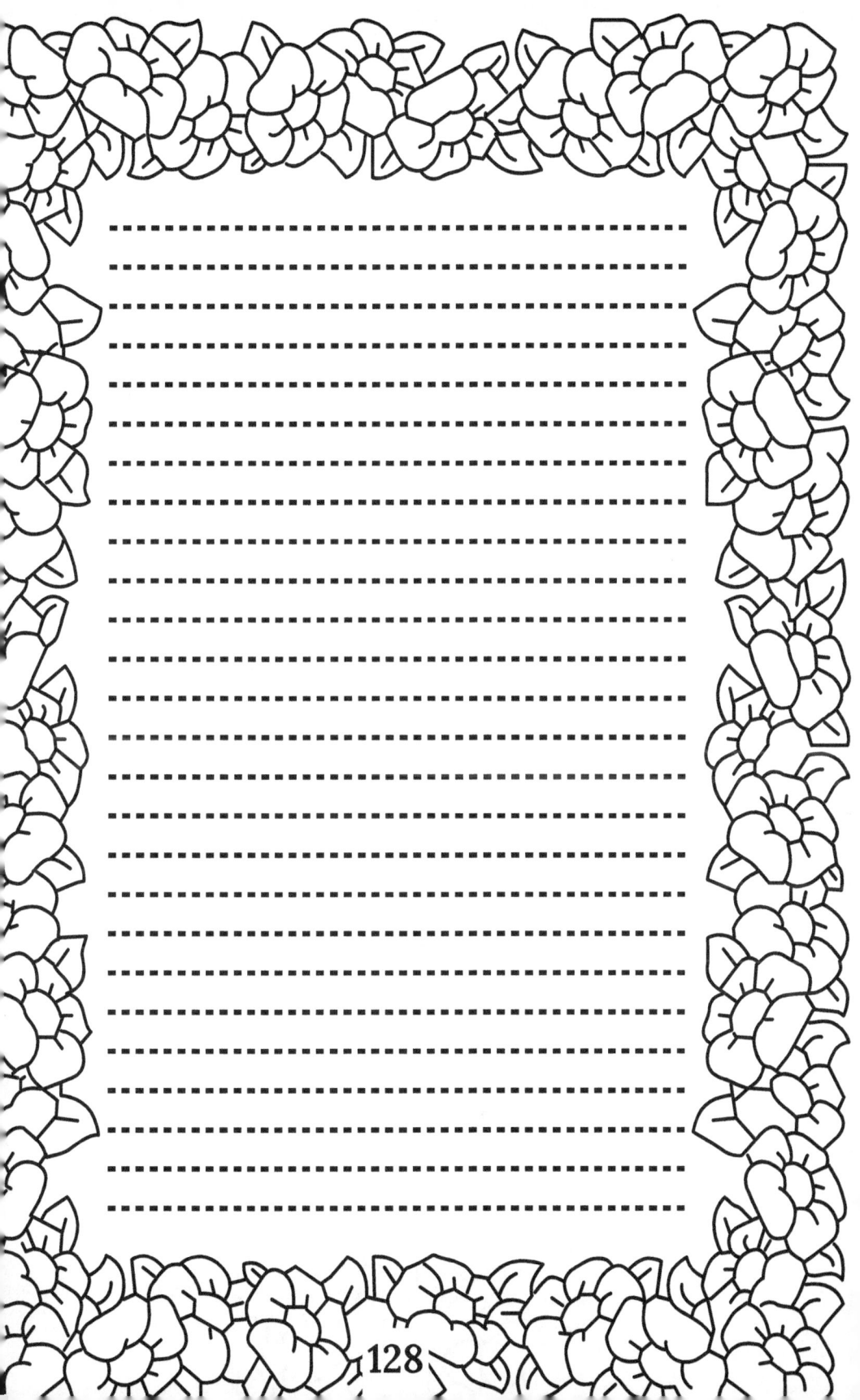

Dear Beautiful Soul,

Congratulations on completing "Soul Wounds: The Ties That Bind." This journey of reflection and healing is a significant achievement, and you should be proud of the insights you've gained.

As you close this journal, take a moment to consider:

- What have you learned about yourself and your siblings?
- How do you feel about the healing process?
- What intentions will you carry forward?

Remember, healing is an ongoing journey. The growth you've experienced here can strengthen your connections and foster deeper understanding.

Thank you for allowing me to be part of your exploration. May you continue to embrace the ties that bind you to your siblings with love and empathy.

With warm wishes for your journey ahead,
Dr. Kellie Diane
Awareherness: The Power to Know©

Soul Wounds

"The Ties That Bind: A Coloring Journey" is a beautifully crafted companion to the guided journal, designed to enhance your exploration of sibling relationships through the therapeutic art of coloring.It invites you to engage, unwind and reflect fostering mindfulness and emotional healing. Perfect for anyone seeking to enrich their journey of understanding and reconciliation within their family.

THANK YOU

www.ingramcontent.com/pod-product-compliance
Lightning Source LLC
Chambersburg PA
CBHW032059020426
42335CB00011B/412